PARK CITY

ISBN 0-916873-50-1
Library of Congress Number 84-050408

©Copyright 1984 The Weller Institute for the Cure of Design, Inc. No part of this publication may be reproduced in any form without permission in writing from the publisher. Copyright to the photographs shown in this book is held by the various photographers. They may not be reproduced without permission of the individual photographers.

The manuscript was edited, proofed, and checked by John Wiebusch. Type specification was by Chikako Weller. Production was done in Park City and Los Angeles by Chikako and Don Weller.

Type faces are primarily Goudy Old Style with captions and heads in the Goudy Family. The Type was set by Alpha Graphix. Color separations, printing, and binding were done in Tokyo, Japan, by Dai Nippon Printing Company.

Historical information comes from many sources, including the Park City Public Library, The University of Utah Library, and numerous personal interviews. The *Park Record* photo file provided reference for illustrations of the contemporary personalities; the Utah State Historical Society furnished visual reference for the historical personalities. The portraits of Plumbob Walker, Big Bill Bennett, and John the Baptist are drawn from description and imagination.

Friends of this project include Beverly Berman, David Boss, Nancy Fees, Derek McClean, Debby Symonds, Jim and Ann Van Noy, Susan Wiebusch, Barron Wolman of Square Books, everyone at Alpha Graphix, and many others.

Published by

The Weller Institute
for the Cure of Design, Inc.
1398 Aerie Drive
P.O. Box 726
Park City, Utah 84060

PARK CITY

WRITTEN BY
KATHERINE REYNOLDS

PHOTOGRAPHS BY
PAT MCDOWELL
NICK NASS
NEIL ROSSMILLER
TOM SHANER

ILLUSTRATED AND
DESIGNED BY
DON WELLER

PRODUCED AND
PUBLISHED BY
**THE WELLER
INSTITUTE FOR THE
CURE OF DESIGN**

PARK CITY

Katherine Reynolds, author, began her writing career after graduating from Northwestern University School of Journalism. Settling in Washington, D.C., she wrote for *Washingtonian* magazine and *The Washington Post* and worked in public information for several federal government agencies.

By the time Katherine moved to Park City, in 1979, she also had acquired a master's degree in public administration at the University of Southern California and was working as a management consultant and training specialist for state and local governments. During her first year in Park City, her consulting included work for the City of San Diego; the City of Saginaw, Mich.; the State of Texas; the U.S. Department of Housing and Urban Development; and the Bureau of Indian Affairs.

Katherine settled in Park City on a full-time basis in 1981 when she and Teri Gomes founded Friday Communications, a public relations firm. While Friday Communications represented clients in Park City and Salt Lake City, Katherine also continued her free-lance writing career. She is the author of a book, *People, Performance... Results*, and the editor of several other books. Her magazine articles have appeared in *Good Housekeeping, American Way, Odyssey, Westways, Historic Preservation, International Management, Working Woman,* and others. Park City readers know her work best by her contributions to *Lodestar*, the bi-annual Park City magazine.

While writing this book, Katherine also was working for the University of Utah as an administrator in the Political Science Department and an instructor in the Department of Communications. She was involved in numerous activities in Park City at the same time, including co-authorship (with David Fleisher and Mike Phillips) of the centennial musical, "This Is The Place", and serving on the Board of Adjustments and the Board of the Park City Community Clinic.

Pat McDowell, photographer, has been a resident of Park City for more than ten years. He is perhaps best known for capturing some of the finest moments in skiing competition and enjoyment on the Park City slopes. An avid skier and wind surfer, Pat is the official photographer for the Park City Ski Area, and runs his own photography service.

In recent years, Pat has photographed the Equitable Ski Challenge, the Grand Marnier Ski Challenge, the U.S. Open Tennis Tournament, and the Equitable Life Insurance tournament. His photographs have appeared in numerous Park City publicity materials and brochures and in publications such as *Ski, Skiing, Powder, Rocky Mountain Skier's Guide, Diversion, Windsurf Magazine, American Showcase, Working Woman,* and *Historic Preservation*.

Nicholas J. Nass, photographer, operates the Powder Room Photo Service at the Park City Resort Center. He shoots both stills and film and accompanies groups, individuals, and race competitors to photograph them on the ski slopes.

Nick graduated with a bachelor of professional arts from Brooks Institute of Photography and also holds a certificate in cinematography from Brooks. He also attended Weber State College and Santa Barbara City College. From 1975 to 1979, he owned and operated Main Street Photographer in Park City. During that time he established the Kimball Art Center's photo department, produced the first Park City Photo Festival, and taught University of Utah-accredited classes at the Art Center.

Nick's long list of published photo credits includes photographs in *Time, Sports Illustrated, Ski, Skiing, Powder, Architectural Digest, MountainWest, Lodestar, and Appaloosa News*. Additional credits and clients have included advertising agencies, large and small companies, government agencies, and non-profit groups. He also has worked as chief photographer for the International Recreational Development Corporation, as manager-instructor for Nord Photo Engineering Color Workshop, and as an honorary instructor of photography for the University of Utah.

Neil G. Rossmiller, photographer, moved to Park City in 1981 and soon opened Park City Black and White, his photographic service and studio. His initial experience in photography began in 1975, when he started a three-year stint working in a camera repair shop in Rock Island, Illinois.

After his camera repair job, Neil worked for the Federal Aviation Administration as an air traffic controller. Following the controllers' strike, he again picked up his cameras. His Utah credits for published photography include photographs in the U.S. Ski Team's Year Book; the Park City Ski Area's Information Guide; the book *Best of the West*, published by the Utah Travel Council; and various literature of the Park City Chamber of Commerce/Convention and Visitors Bureau. Neil's photographic specialties include action, sports, outdoor scenes, and architecture.

Tom Shaner, photographer, works in Park City as both a photographer and a senior draftsman and land planner for Deer Valley. Born and raised in Michigan, Tom moved to Park City in 1977.

Tom's first photographic work was with an old Miranda Range Finder camera given to him by his mother-in-law. An admitted "self-taught photographer", he went on to specialize in photographing advertising and commercial sets, products, architecture, and outdoor scenes. He works in 35 mm and large format (4 x 5).

Tom graduated from Kendall School of Design, Grand Rapids, Michigan. His photographs have appeared in *California* magazine, public relations and advertising literature for Deer Valley Resort and real estate in Deer Valley, and materials of the Park City Chamber of Commerce/Visitor and Convention Bureau.

Don Weller, designer and illustrator, is in partnership with his wife, Chikako, in the Weller Institute for the Cure of Design, Inc. Their business creates trademarks, brochures, posters, packages, and illustrations; it has been featured in articles in design magazines, including *Communication Arts* and *Idea*.

Born too late to be a real cowboy, Don tried his hand at rodeo competition and studied at Washington State University, graduating with a degree in Fine Arts. He moved to Los Angeles and went into the graphic design business. In addition to maintaining his own office, he taught design at University of California, Los Angeles, and illustration at the Art Center College of Design.

Currently, Don and Chikako reside parttime in Park City, leaving Los Angeles for the ski slopes and clean air. With two colleagues, Don sponsors "The Design Conference That Just Happens To Be In Park City" for designers who want to ski.

Don has won many awards, including gold medals from the New York Art Directors Club and the New York One Show, as well as the Los Angeles Society of Illustrators Lifetime Achievement Award.

CONTRIBUTORS

PARK CITY

1847	Brigham Young and his Mormon pioneers settle in the Salt Lake Valley.
1868	Soldiers from Colonel Patrick Conner's troops at Camp Douglas discover silver ore near Park City.
1872	The mine camp is formally named "Park City" in Fourth of July ceremonies.
1884	Park City is granted its official Charter of Incorporation.
1898	The "Great Fire" destroys 75 percent of Park City's buildings.
1919	The Walsh-Pittman Act sets a minimum price for silver, bringing a new mining upsurge to Park City.
1929	The "Crash" brings plummeting silver prices and mine closures.
1946	Park City's first ski lift, "Snow Park," is built in Deer Valley.
1962	The federal government loans $1.2 million to United Park City Mines to develop a ski area.
1963	The "Treasure Mountain Resort," later to expand to the Park City Ski Area, opens.
1981	A second major resort, Deer Valley, opens in Park City's boundaries.

THE CHRONOLOGY

PARK CITY

Bald Mountain Flagstaff Mountain Jupiter Peak

Deer Valley   Park City   Resort Center   Park West

THE MOUNTAINS

PARK CITY

Page title	Photograph description	Photographer

The bold numbers indicate individual photographs on a page, reading left to right and top to bottom.

Dust cover (front)	Stein Eriksen in fresh powder, Deer Valley. *Pat McDowell*	
Dust cover (back)	Box elder leaves. *Pat McDowell*	
Full page	Skier Dave Parker jumping off No Punk Rock in McConkey's Bowl. *Neil Rossmiller*	
Spread	Jupiter Peak from American Flag. *Tom Shaner*	
High powder	**1** Mountain peaks. *Pat McDowell* **2** Weasel of Park City ski bum fame. White Pine between Park City and Park West. *Pat McDowell* **3** The Ridge at White Pine. *Pat McDowell* **4** Wasatch Powder Guides at the top of Homelight: going home. *Pat McDowell* **5** Chopper skiing, Park City back country. *Pat McDowell* **6** Karen Scheer at Jupiter Bowl. *Pat McDowell*	
Full page	Stein Eriksen through the aspens at Deer Valley. *Pat McDowell*	
Fast slopes	**1, & 2** NOR AM's NCAA racing at Park City. Young Olympic hopefuls. *Pat McDowell* **3** Women's professional skiing at Park West. *Pat McDowell* **4, 5, & 6** Pro ski racing. *Pat McDowell* **7** Downhill. *Karen Scheer*	
Full page	Bumping at Park City. *Pat McDowell*	
Alpine	**1, 2, 3, & 4** World pro skiing. *Nick Nass*	
Nordic	NCAA Nordic competition at Deer Park. *Pat McDowell*	
Soaring	**1** Blasting skier. *Pat McDowell* **2** Craig Badami performing snow analysis at the Greater Park City Ski Resort. *Pat McDowell* **3** Stewart Campbell, 72, skiing with two young friends. *Pat McDowell*	
Smiling	**1** Girl. *Neil Rossmiller* **2** The Bedder brothers getting air on Thaynes. *Pat McDowell* **3** Girl. *Neil Rossmiller* **4** Girl. *Neil Rossmiller* **5** Women's pro skiing competitor at Park West. *Pat McDowell* **6** Dave Bodner making it safe. *Pat McDowell* **7** Kinderschool. *Pat McDowell* **8** Tina Quail, Park City Ski Resort hostess (in Deer Valley hat). *Neil Rossmiller* **9** Spring spectating. *Neil Rossmiller* **10** Karen tree skiing. *Pat McDowell* **11** Bitten Eriksen, Stein's mother, still knitting and skiing. *Pat McDowell*	
Full page	The dairy barn between Ridgeview and Park West. Park West is in the background. *Don Weller*	
Eagles View	The Park City Resort, Silver Queen, Crescent, Silver Skies, the runs, and Park City in the foreground. The view from the Aerie. *Don Weller*	
Spread	Snow-covered dogwoods near Park West. *Tom Shaner*	
Snow cover	**1** Snow-covered roof, Prospector Square area. *Don Weller* **2** Red Banjo Pizza Parlor and full moon. *Tom Shaner* **3** Condo roof, Park West. *Don Weller* **4** Horse near Park Meadows. *Don Weller* **5** Volkswagen bug in the snow in old town. Street mogul. *Nick Nass* **6** Old town and Deer Valley's Bald Mountain at dusk, the view from the Aerie. *Don Weller* **7** Moonlit Silver Lake Lodge, Deer Valley. *Tom Shaner* **8** Railroad car, Skyline Land Company. *Don Weller*	
Snow cover (continued)	**1** Victorian gingerbread. *Don Weller* **2** Sunspot condos, Sunnyside, between Park City and Deer Valley. *Don Weller* **3** Coalition mine building. *Nick Nass* **4** Skating at the Resort Center. *Don Weller* **5** Old mine structure, Thaynes Canyon. *Tom Shaner* **6** Approaching storm, Park City. *Tom Shaner* **7** Rossi Hill in the moonlight. *Tom Shaner* **8** Railroad car, the Union Pacific. *Don Weller* **9** Park City's railroad station. *Don Weller*	
Evolving	**1** Wooden bullwheel inside the coalition mine building. *Pat McDowell* **2** The coalition mine building, for many years the symbol of Park City, in autumn. *Pat McDowell* **3** Three Kings condominium on the Park City golf course. *Pat McDowell* **4** The old Miner's Hospital on Park Avenue, now the public library. *Neil Rossmiller* **5** The Silver Queen at the bottom of Main Street. *Pat McDowell* **6** House in old town. *Neil Rossmiller* **7** The National Garage and other weathering typography on Park Avenue. *Don Weller* **8** The Egyptian Theater. *Pat McDowell*	
Evolving (continued)	**1** Autumn fog. *Tom Shaner* **2** Stein Eriksen Lodge. *Tom Shaner* **3** Old tools. *Pat McDowell* **4** Graves of miners and others. *Nick Nass*	
Backward forward	**1** Old town and Saint Mary's Catholic Church. *Nick Nass* **2** Mine camp from Rossi Hill. *Tom Shaner* **3** Roof detail. *Pat McDowell*	
Full page	Dairy barn and rainbow. *Nick Nass*	
Spread	Balloons, Autumn Aloft, Park Meadows. *Neil Rossmiller*	

ABOUT THE PHOTOGRAPHS

PARK CITY

Warm and wet	1	Autumn Aloft. *Pat McDowell*
	2	Ed Pouquette on the course. *Pat McDowell*
	3	The Park City golf course. *Pat McDowell*
	4 & 5	Jet, a member of the winning team, Park City Ride and Tie. *Neil Rossmiller*
	6	Waiting for the wind, boards to rent. *Pat McDowell*
	7	Windsurfing. Deer Creek Regatta. *Pat McDowell*
	8	Ducks at Deer Creek. *Neil Rossmiller*
Warm and wet (continued)	1	Horseback riding in the high country. *Pat McDowell*
	2	Rugby. Park City Muckers vs Snake River. The Annual Rugby Challenge Cup. *Pat McDowell*
	3	BMX (Bicycle Motocross). Hot and taking off. *Pat McDowell*
	4	Striker the cat lives with Neil Rossmiller on King Road. *Neil Rossmiller*
	5	Tennis anyone? *Pat McDowell*
	6	Trout fishing. *Pat McDowell*
Country roads	1	Beaver work on the aspen trees in Guardsmans Pass behind Jupiter Bowl. *Neil Rossmiller*
	2	Mountain lane, the ski-in access to Stein Eriksen Lodge. *Tom Shaner*
	3	Autumn on Bald Mountain. View of the Camas Valley. *Tom Shaner*
Flora	1	Apple blossoms. *Neil Rossmiller*
	2	Horse trail. *Tom Shaner*

	3	White flower. *Neil Rossmiller*
	4	California poppy. *Tom Shaner*
	5	Choke cherries. *Pat McDowell*
	6	Scrub oak in color and an old fence. *Neil Rossmiller*
	7	Hens and chicks blossom. *Neil Rossmiller*
	8	Indian paintbrush. *Tom Shaner*
	9	Blue columbine. *Tom Shaner*
	10	Philadelphia fleabane. *Tom Shaner*
	11	Bluebell. *Neil Rossmiller*
	12	Miner's delight. The miners picked this and put it in their pillows. The menthol smell helped ease the symptoms of black lung. *Pat McDowell*
Fauna	1	Jack rabbit. *Nick Nass*
	2	Hawk. *Nick Nass*
	3	Black-capped chickadee eating hop seeds. *Neil Rossmiller*
	4	Bobcat. *Nick Nass*
	5	Pine martin in Summit Park. *Neil Rossmiller*
	6	Raccoon. *Nick Nass*
	7, 8, & 9	Deer. *Nick Nass*
Full page		Aspens, Park City ski resort. *Neil Rossmiller*
Spread		Red scrub oak. *Tom Shaner*
Think snow	1	Autumn leaves. *Nick Nass*
	2	Quaking aspens. *Pat McDowell*

ABOUT THE PHOTOGRAPHS

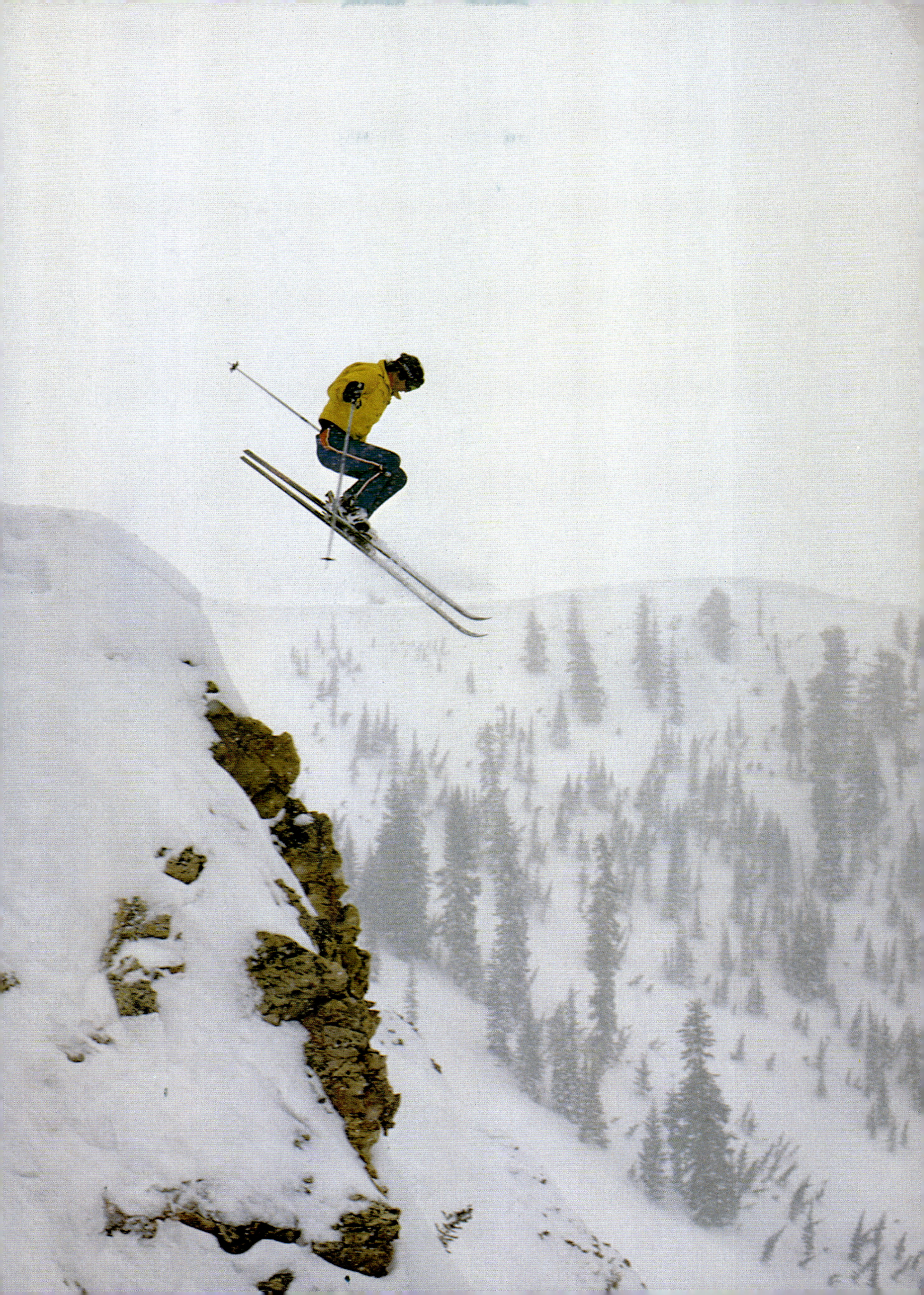

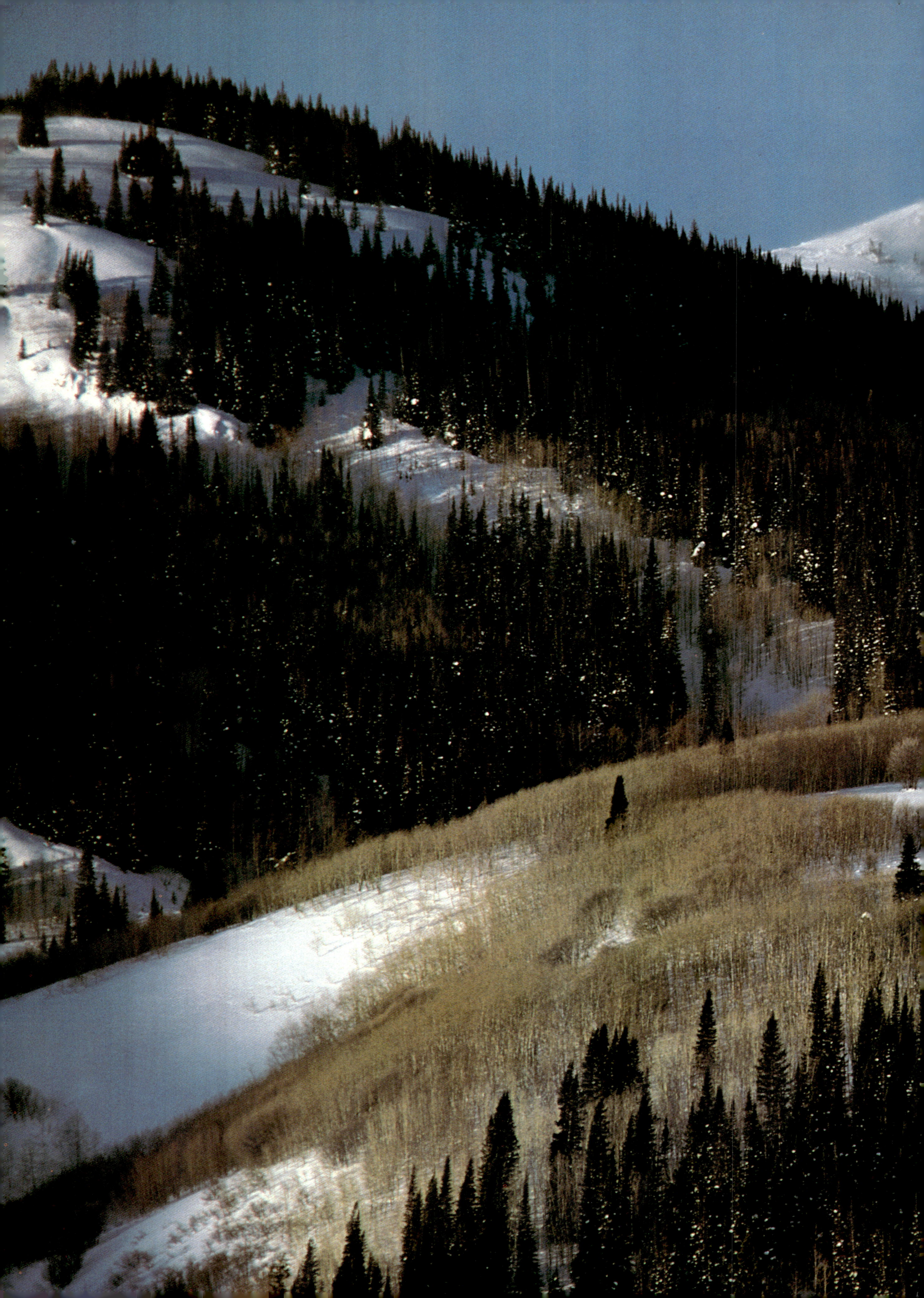

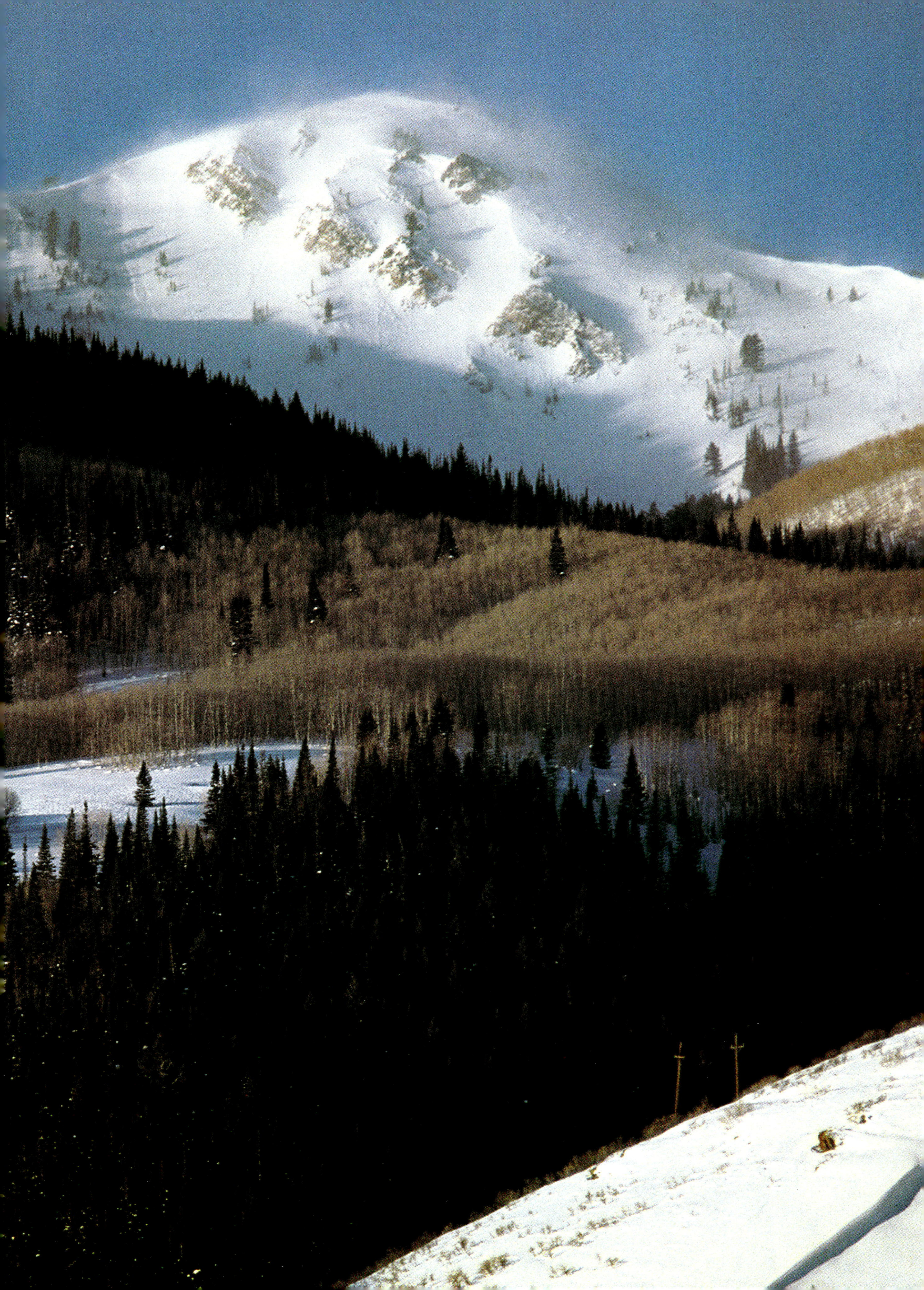

PARK CITY

With an annual average snowfall of approximately 300 inches, Park City is well blanketed with the Utah powder called, "the greatest snow on earth."

HIGH POWDER

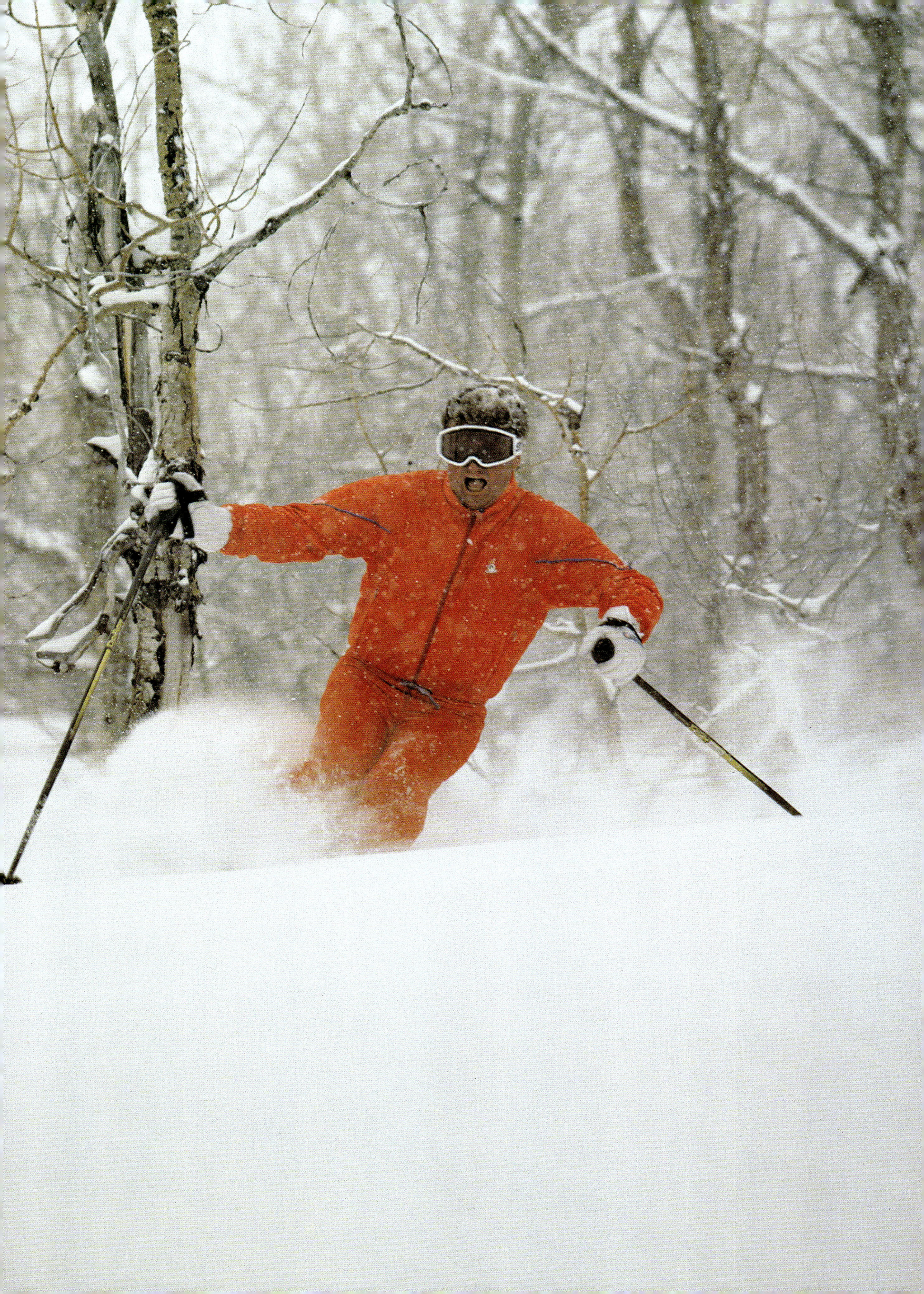

PARK CITY

The three ski resorts in the Park City area host dozens of local and national races each year. Park City is headquarters for the United States Ski Team.

FAST SLOPES

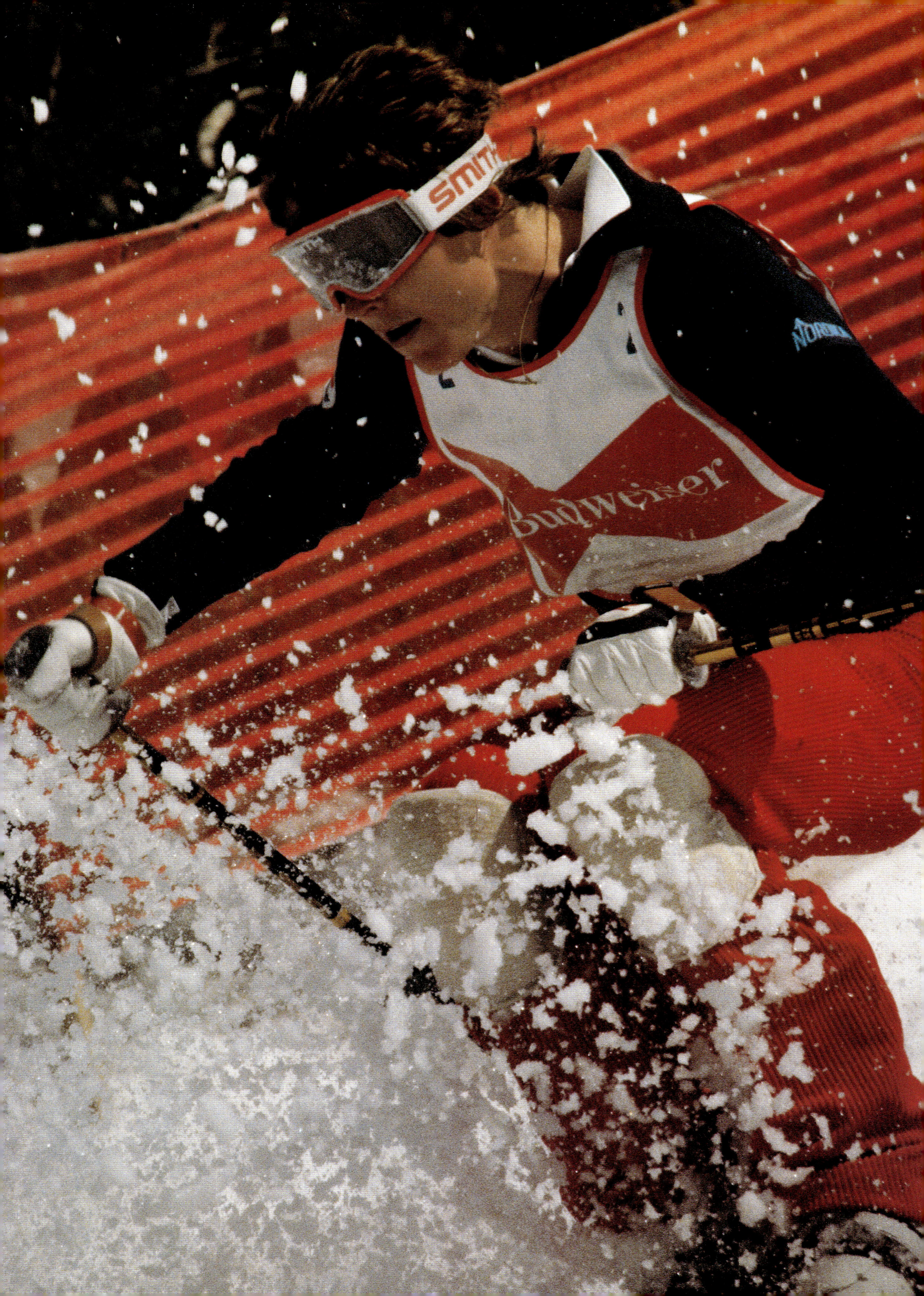
SMITH
Budweiser

P A R K   C I T Y

A L P I N E

PARK CITY

NORDIC

P A R K C I T Y

Skiing is enjoyed by hearty athletes and hearty spectators alike. Take to the high country... take a leap... take off....

S O A R I N G

PARK CITY

SMILING

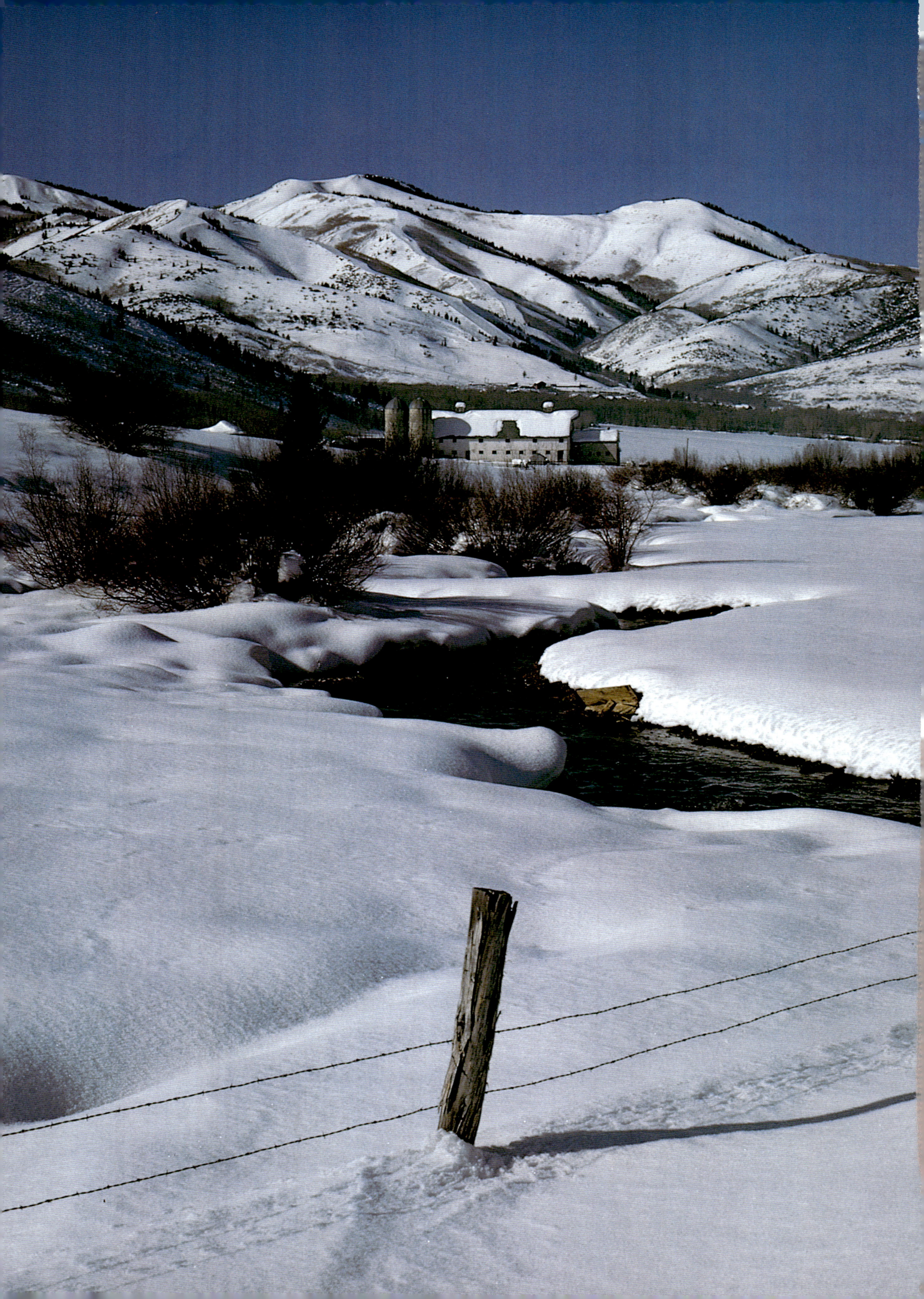

PARK CITY

Mine camp, turned boomtown, turned ghost town, turned ski resort: This is the stuff of Park City's hundred-year evolution.

Booms and busts, riches and rags, good times and hard times: All are part of the town's checkered past. But if there is a theme in Park City's patchwork history, it is not simply found in the growth of silver mining and the advent of skiing. It is better defined as the struggle of the town and its citizens to build and maintain a community identity in the face of difficult odds. From the beginning, Park City was exposed to the same boomtown syndrome that turned most western mine camps from fabled to forgotten almost overnight.

Typical of many old mining communities, great wealth was accumulated in Park City and then quickly taken away. Mine moguls Thomas Kearns and David Keith made their millions from the tunnels under "the Park," but built their mansions and contributed to their charities down the canyon in Salt Lake City. John Judge's mining bonanza built a hospital, and, later, a school in Salt Lake City; and the Hearst family empire multiplied in Park City, but kept California as home. No schools, hospitals, parks, or municipal buildings in Park City bear the names of those who made their fortunes there.

It was the miners' union that spearheaded a fund drive to erect Park City's hospital in 1904. Subscriptions from all segments of the community built the Grand Opera House, and the local churches established the early schools. Land for a city cemetery was donated by a pioneer father who had buried his infant daughter on his own property and later deeded the site to the town. Thus, Park City established a tradition of community contribution that probably is responsible for its survival.

Unfortunately, the individuals often most responsible for the plain but important work of community building rarely are the personalities whose names survive when historical legends and adventures are recounted. But they were there for Park City, and the history that follows owes a debt of gratitude to them...

BACK THEN

PARK CITY

Colonel Connor caught a chronic case of gold and silver fever himself and frequently took time from Army duties to prospect with his men.

Park City old-timers always have recounted the "Great Fire of 1898" with the sort of reverence people in Virginia and Georgia generally reserve for the defeated Confederacy. A mining boom town was ablaze on that early morning in June, while hard work, hopes, and homes became the kindling consumed by the flames crackling down Main Street. Churches, opera houses, hotels, homes, and business establishments crumbled into ashes, and fire fighters and citizen volunteers quickly lost the blistering battle against the wind-swept inferno.

Maybe it was humor born of unspeakable tragedy. Maybe it was hysteria in the midst of danger. Whatever the motivation, Fred Jenning's response to the fire was quite unexpected. He rolled a piano into the street and began a spontaneous outdoor concert with "There'll Be A Hot Time In The Old Town Tonight."

By 1898, however, Park City residents had been well schooled to expect the unexpected and accept the eccentric. After all, it had taken a good dose of rugged individualism to carve a town 7,000 feet high in the desolate Wasatch range, a span of jagged peaks marked by certain winter brutality and uncertain prospects of underground silver and gold. Indians had roamed on through the area without pitching any permanent tepees; Spanish explorers had kept to the south; and Brigham Young had chosen the lower valley to the West when he proclaimed, "This is the place," to Utah's Mormon settlers of 1847.

The mountains surrounding Park City became the province of a different breed of characters during the late Nineteenth Century. Risk takers, fun seekers, and escapists were as at home as the hobos, Bohemians, and hippies of later generations. They were an eclectic lot, long on bravado and short on pessimism. Men such as Solon Spiro, who spoke only German when he arrived in Park City in 1894 to work in his uncle's mercantile store, but who quickly amassed and lost a fortune in mining investments. Women such as "Trixie" and "Frisco," who plyed their profession in the town's red light district. Miners such as Frank O'Hara, accustomed to trudging to work in waist-deep snow but who became one of numerous avalanche fatalities during the horrible winter of 1886. Entrepreneurs such as Susanna Emery-Holmes, Utah's famed and flamboyant "Silver Queen," whose world-wide travels and lavish entertainment outlasted her four marriages and a $100 million fortune.

Lumber and farming had brought the first settlers to the Park City area. They had little thought of the underground ore riches that soon would produce a mining boom. Halfway through the Nineteenth Century, the California gold rush still was the siren for prospecting hopefuls. Mormon settler Parley Pratt, who came up from the Salt Lake Valley to graze cattle in the flat land just north of Park City, amassed a windfall by building a toll road that meandered toward Salt Lake City. In 1850, fortune seekers who were on their way to California paid $1,500 to use Pratt's route.

Another Mormon pioneer, Samuel Snyder, also soon moved up from the Valley to the area that would become known as Parley's Park. After purchasing "squatter's rights" from Pratt in 1853 for a yoke of oxen, he started a thriving sawmill in the midst of hearty mountain timbers. Like Pratt, Snyder's attention was focused on the Salt Lake Valley settlement, where he milled and sold lumber to keep pace with the growing Mormon settlement. Pratt and Snyder soon were joined by fellow Mormons Heber Kimball and Jedediah Grant, enlarging the Parley's Park settlement to hamlet proportions.

The United States government, uneasy about possible Mormon unrest while the Civil War raged back East, also focused a certain amount of attention on the Salt Lake Valley area. Colonel Patrick E. Connor was identified as the right man for the job of keeping an eye on the Mormons and soon became the first of many memorable characters to contribute to the rise of a mining settlement high in the Wasatch mountains.

In 1862, Connor and some 300 California and Nevada volunteers founded Camp Douglas (later Fort Douglas) in the foothills above Salt Lake City. The mustachioed, mutton-chopped Connor immediately proved more innovative and ambitious than the popular conception of the Army man. With an eye toward the possibilities of silver and gold hidden in the rocky terrain, he urged his troops to prospect in their spare time. An 1863 edition of Camp Douglas' *Union Vedette* newspaper carried Connor's

---

THE SETTLERS

PARK CITY

personal announcement that, "Miners and prospecting parties will receive the fullest protection from the military forces in this district."

The prospectors had no competition from the Mormon population. Brigham Young had admonished the Mormons by saying, "It is our duty first to develop the agricultural resources of this country. As for gold and silver and other rich minerals of the earth… leave them alone."

Colonel Connor's hot Irish temperament was a classic match for fire and brimstone emanating from Mormon quarters, and a war of words exploded between the military and religious communities. Connor demonstrated his capacity for both theatrics and bigotry when he requested, unsuccessfully, 3,000 additional men from the Army Department. "Suffice it," he wrote his superiors of the Mormons, "I find them a community of traitors, murderers, fanatics, and whores."

Brigham Young was not a man to pull punches or mince words, either. In an 1863 sermon, he characterized the Army presence as, "A view to flood the country with just such a population as they desire, to destroy, if possible, the identity of the Mormon community and every truth and virtue that remains."

The Colonel himself caught a chronic case of gold and silver fever and frequently took time from Army duties to prospect with his men. In fact, his own silver strike in Little Cottonwood Canyon (near the current town of Alta) in 1864 was the first silver discovery in the Wasatch range.

It wasn't until 1869, however, when the golden spike driven near Ogden, Utah, connected the Central Pacific and Union Pacific railroads, that scattered prospecting could advance toward organized mining. That same year, determined prospectors were picking and shoveling their way up the canyon from Parley's Park, just north of Park City. Other hopefuls were converging on the same area from the rugged passes over Big Cottonwood Canyon to the area south of Park City now called Bonanza Flats.

While the enigmatic nature of making strikes and filing claims made it impossible to accurately distinguish the first mining discovery in the Park City area, credit generally is given to three of Connor's soldiers. Exploring the area in 1868, the three pried off an odd-looking outcropping of quartz. Upon further examination, the hunk of rock turned out to be full of silver, lead, and gold. The discovery cinched a certain immortality for the Colonel, who soon came to be known as the "Father of Utah Mining." It marked the crude beginnings of the settlement that became one of the richest mining camps in the country.

Early prospectors gave little thought to building any permanent settlement. Satisfied with the vagabond ways of work that might produce all or nothing, they set up only brush shanties and tents near their diggings—primarily around the the Lake Flat area (now part of Deer Valley). Mormon settlers just to the North, however, contributed goods and services, as well as a penchant for putting down roots, and helped turn the mine camp into a permanent settlement in spite of itself—an ironic turn of events considering the wide chasm between values and attitudes held by the Mormons and the miners.

George G. Snyder, another unique character of early Park City, was as responsible as anyone for helping the mining camp become a real community. After all, even before this Mormon bishop moved to the scrappy settlement, he had demonstrated a certain flair for nesting by taking five wives.

Born in New York, George migrated to Utah in 1849, a year after his brother Samuel. He settled in Wanship, 10 miles north of his brother's sawmill at Parley's Park. As the mining camp grew, George weighed the opportunities for starting a new life there. Finally, in 1872, he packed his fifth wife, Rhoda, and their two young children, Lillie and Kimball, into his wagon and set out along the rocky trails. It only may have been a 10-mile trip to Park City, but most of it was through heavy sage brush and over jagged rocks. George had to stop often to hack away brush in the path and give his heavy, horse-drawn wagon an extra push over the steepest sections.

Legend has it that the Snyder family was responsible for many "firsts" in the settlement, not the least of which was the first time the area was referred to as "Park City." Prior to the Snyders' arrival, it had been known as Upper Parley's and Upper Kimball, after the prominent Mormon settlers. Some even had called it Mineral City. After their rough wagon haul to the area, the Snyder family finally reached the meadows opening on the mine camp settlement. Eyeing the sage and wildflowers, George turned to Rhoda and exclaimed, "This is a veritable park. We will call this place Park City." Or so the legend goes.

Other, less inspired, tales of the naming of Park City

THE SETTLERS

PARK CITY

Eying the sage and wildflowers, George Snyder turned to his fifth wife, Rhoda, and exclaimed, "This is a veritable park. We will call this place Park City." Or so the legend goes.

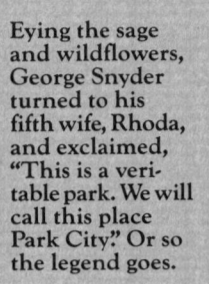

include the rather logical explanation that since Parley's Park already was a nearby farming settlement, locals simply began calling the mine camp Parley's Park City, which later was shortened to Park City. At any rate, there is general agreement that during a home spun flag raising ceremony on July 4, 1872, the settlers formally declared their camp to be "Park City."

George and Rhoda Snyder soon selected a homesite, just across Park Avenue from the current Kimball Art Center, and used abundant local logs to construct the first house in Park City. They later enlarged their home to become a boarding house for miners, who knew Rhoda as "Aunt Rhoda" for her cooking talents, nursing abilities, and cheerful hospitality.

Struggle was a way of life for these early homesteaders, who pitted themselves against cruel winters and dry summers. In 1877, Rhoda gave birth to their daughter Pearle, the first child born in Park City. In 1879, Pearle was also Park City's first fatality, after contracting a fever at a time when high snows defeated all attempts to reach doctors in Salt Lake City. The Snyders did try to take Pearle's tiny body to Salt Lake City for burial, hitching their horses to a sleigh carrying a hand-made pine casket. The horses made little progress through the belly-deep snow and were stopped completely at the junction to Heber. There, George scratched out a shallow grave on a south-facing slope and buried his daughter on his own land. Later, he deeded the property to the city for use as a permanent municipal cemetery.

Silver mining brought Park City to the fever pitch of the lucrative activity for which it was known best in the late Nineteenth Century. Men who rode into town with nothing struck a vein and a deal, pocketed a fortune, and left. Men of great wealth sent money to Park City for further investment and reclaimed it after it had multiplied hundreds-fold. The once-lush forests covering the mountain slopes were cut down to make the mine tunnels and town structures.

Risk takers and mavericks joined in to cast their lot on dreams of the big discovery. Irish potato famine survivors opened saloons and restaurants, Chinese railroad workers opened laundries, Cornish copper miners opened a maze of underground tunnels, and Scandinavian loggers opened the thick forests to provide construction wood. By the 1890s, 40 percent of the town's population was foreign-born.

One talented entrepreneur who wasted no time getting in on the Park City bonanza was George Hearst, father of publishing magnate William Randolph Hearst. A veteran of the Comstock Lode rush and the primary force behind a silver boom in Cortez, Nevada, Hearst already was investing in some southern Utah mines when he heard of riches to the north.

With his southern Utah mine manager, Robert Craig (R.C.) Chambers, Hearst began poking around Park City in 1872 for worthy investments. The first strike already had led to continuous ore shipments from the Flagstaff Mine, and an even larger silver and lead operation was underway at the nearby McHenry Mine. New claims were being staked nearly every day, and Hearst was determined to buy or discover a mine in the area.

Chambers personally examined the McHenry shaft, but advised Hearst against buying that mine due to accumulating water that continually slowed the digging progress. A clever and cunning fellow — some later would call his business practices "downright slimy" — Chambers kept up the search for a worthy Hearst investment until he stumbled on some recent discoveries just over the next ridge on Ontario Ledge. There, he found Herman Buden, Rector Steen, James Kane, and Augustus Dawell busily digging around an ore vein they had discovered only a few days before. The silver not only looked good, but proved to assay for $200 per ton. Within a month, the fledgling vein belonged to Hearst, at a $27,000 purchase price. Within 15 years, Hearst's profits from the Ontario Mine had mounted to $9 million; by the time it closed in 1897, the big vein had produced more than $50 million in ore. So pure was the Ontario ore that its tailings were worked another seven years after the mine closed.

The water-plagued McHenry, which Chambers had passed up, didn't do badly either. A silver rich tunnel just below the level Chambers had examined eventually yielded $15 million in ore for the Park Utah Mining Company. Still, one good decision was enough to set Chambers up as a wealthy Hearst corporate manager and wily wheeler dealer in Park City for years to come. A Missouri native, purveyor of that distinct "show me" skepticism, the long-faced and bearded mine manager was ever ready to step on anything or anyone who came between him and the Hearst mine interests.

BOOM TOWN

PARK CITY

For years, the Ontario Silver Mining Company was the major economic force in Park City, and Chambers was the prime mover behind every significant mining deal. Mine laborer John Daly surprised the town by quietly buying title to 24 claims in Empire Canyon, just west of the Ontario operations. But when his explorations resulted in a healthy 800-ton-per-month production and half of that was deeded to Chambers, there was no doubt who Daly's backer had been.

Nor did civic mindedness ever interfere with the machinations of the aloof, generally ill-liked Chambers. When a group of wealthy mine investors from Michigan decided to apply to the state government of Utah for a formal "townsite" for Park City, the early settlers who already lived on the future townsite were appalled at the thought of surrendering their buildings or buying back their "squatters-rights" land from newcomers. But their cause was lost quickly after Chambers suddenly added his power and influence to assist the townsite proponents in gaining state approval. Shortly after the inevitable payments and surrendering actions by furious "locals", Chambers showed up with title to a millsite for the Ontario within townsite boundaries. Popular speculation was that the title had been his reward for supporting the Michigan newcomers at the expense of original settlers.

Heavy-handedness became Chambers' trademark. When he suspected the mining operation adjacent to the Ontario was taking ore from his mine, he had his men force out the neighboring miners by blasting tar and sulpher into their tunnels. He often accused Jack Smith, the owner of another adjacent claim, of tunneling into Ontario property, but to no avail. Chambers then hired a tough new employee, Jack Moray; a few days later, Moray picked an argument with Smith in a local saloon and shot and killed him. Although Smith had been unarmed, the skillful Ontario attorneys managed to get Moray off with only 18 months in prison.

While the plain folk had no love lost for Chambers, they could not deny that his empire building for the Ontario had made mining history and put Park City on the map—an act that took place officially on March 8, 1884, when the state of Utah granted a charter of incorporation to the mine camp that had grown to more than 4,000 permanent residents in only 20 years.

In fact, the mine camp had taken on the look of a small city well before incorporation. By 1874, Main Street had become the obvious center, complete with a general merchandise store, a blacksmith shop, a saloon, a meat market, and a boarding house, all scattered among some log residences and brush shanties. Six years later, a Park City Business Directory listed five saloons, three general merchandise stores, two butchers, two livery stables, a post office, and two physicians. A home dramatic society was formed in 1880, bringing a bit of culture to the camp, and it soon was followed by a debating society, a concert band, and a brass band. A Victorian city hall was erected in 1884 to house the new city government and a territorial jail, and Society Hall was built to accommodate elaborate stage shows, operas, dances, and concerts.

Schools and churches also kept pace with the growing community. St. Mary's, the first Catholic church in Utah, was built in 1881, followed shortly by St. Luke's Episcopal Church. Practicing Mormons, an unpopular minority in the booming and often bawdy town, met only in private homes during this period. However, the local newspaper estimated that their numbers reached "several scores" by the 1890s. A free school was established in 1879, and St. Mary's formed a Catholic school in 1881. The Congregational school, which was called Park City Academy, the Ontario Mine District School, and the Methodist school were in business by 1884; at the same time, the public school added popular adult education at night with courses from reading to sewing.

The *Park Record*, Park City's weekly newspaper, under the stewardship of crusty editor Sam Raddon, added yet another dimension to educating the populace in 1884—or, at least it educated them to the thoughts of Sam Raddon,

> Sam Raddon's editorials were so outspoken that they even became the subject of editorials in other Utah newspapers. An 1887 edition of the *Provo Territorial Enquirer* fumed, "The *Park Record* has got the Mormon rabies bad…"

BOOM TOWN

PARK CITY

a strongly opinionated man. Raddon cast a bushy-browed eye on Park City activities for the next 65 years. It often was a disapproving—even prejudiced—eye; Raddon took pot shots at Mormons and applauded when one of the first official government ordinances forbade Chinese laundries to operate on Main Street.

But the *Record* was more soap box than scandal sheet, and it did report the news. The rationale for the *Record's* homespun style and tone probably was best described in Raddon's February 11, 1899, editorial celebrating the paper's nineteenth anniversary (the original newspaper had begun in 1880):

"The *Record* ...has worked incessantly for the best interests of the town and its inhabitants, never wavering in its advocacy of every worthy enterprise and never hesitating to condemn where condemnation was deserved. That the paper has erred many times and many a time we fully realize, but to err is human, and the *Record* is just as apt to get off occasionally as any ordinary mortal."

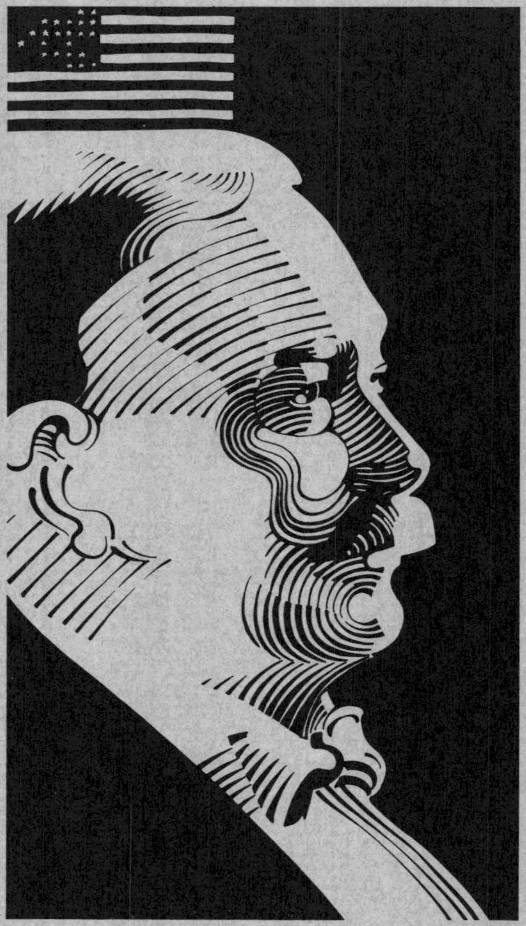

Raddon's *Park Record* not only reported, it interpreted, debated, decided, scolded, and commented, often embellishing news stories with its own brand of editorial opinion. A murder/suicide by a local livery owner who shot his wife and then himself immediately was reported as "premeditated" and with "proof of intent"—well before any official investigation. When a young prostitute died in 1897, the *Park Record's* obituary referred to her as "a resident of Park City's immoral districts," and mentioned pointedly that, "her erring sisters took up a collection to defray funeral expenses."

The most caustic side of Raddon's tongue, however, was reserved for Park City's Chinese and Mormon residents. Since these groups were distinct minorities, shunned by much of Park City's mining elite and European descendants, Raddon had plenty of support when he referred to the Chinese as "Chinks" and "heathens," and equal support when he urged the ousting of Mormons so Park City could become "the only gentile town in Utah." The Mormons already felt compelled to hold quiet services in the privacy of each others' homes; and the community had built a bridge over its Chinatown section just behind Main Street, so that residents on the ridge to the east (called Rossi Hill because it was populated by a group from Rossi, New York) could avoid passing through the Chinese section on trips to and from the business district.

Raddon's editorials were so outspoken that they even became the subject of editorials in other Utah newspapers. In an 1887 edition of the *Provo Territorial Enquirer*, its editor fumed, "The *Park Record* has got the Mormon rabies bad, and is proving itself a complete ass. Poor thing, it is a financial fizzle and thinks it may make a living catering to the tastes of the anti Mormons."

Of course, there also was plenty of fair, if frank, criticism after Raddon attended shows at the Grand Opera House or Society Hall, where residents were entertained by shows ranging from Buffalo Bill Cody to Zimlock the Magician. When prize fighter John L. Sullivan acted in a stage production in Park City, Raddon asserted, "He is a far better fighter than he is an actor!"

In those days, a colorful character such as Raddon may not have seemed very remarkable in a town that seemed to attract more than its share of characters. A tall, gangly miner, affectionately known as "John the Baptist," roamed the dirt streets mumbling through his full beard and stopping on street corners to pronounce his own interpretations of the Gospel. Another mining hopeful, known as Plumbob Walker, proclaimed himself the local astrologer and used a carpenter's plumb bob in his constant, if unsuccessful, search for silver. A husband to two wives and father of 21 children, Plumbob eventually was killed by a young hoodlum who shot him as he stepped outside his cabin at the base of Main Street. Outraged, as usual, the *Park Record* called the crime "one of the most cowardly murders that ever occurred in this city," but couldn't resist further mentioning that Plumbob's "mental facilities were not in their normal condition."

Bill Bennett was another notable character. A parttime miner who lived in a dirt floor shack with his wife and six children, he caught fish for family meals by setting off

COMMUNITY BUILDING

dynamite in a nearby stream. When one blast went awry, he lost his right arm. Bennett's real claim to fame was his well-known drinking and brawling in the local saloons. Not that barroom brawls were the least bit unusual in this rowdy town, but Bennett simply was meaner than most when under the influence. In fact, even the local sheriff was reluctant to arrest him when he picked a fight.

Park City not only accepted this ruffian, it found a positive use for him. The local judge, noting the difficulty he was having in keeping a town marshal during the time of rough miners and trigger-happy newcomers, appointed Bill Bennett city marshal. With a sharp hook in place of his right hand and a badge and a gun, Bennett turned his mean streak to the cause of law and order. He terrorized would-be and actual offenders, bringing a new brand of quick and efficient law enforcement to the frontier town.

No doubt, this turn of events pleased *Record* editor Raddon, who in 1887 had written, "There is altogether too much promiscuous shooting in the streets at night." One of the most notorious of these occurred that same year when Black Jack Murphy shot and killed a local miner, Matt Brennan, as Brennan was riding his horse through a brushy canyon to survey his claims. Murphy confessed and was awaiting trial at the county seat jail in Coalville when a mob from Park City commandeered a railroad engine and took it to Coalville. They brought Murphy back and lynched him beside the tracks at Park City's train depot.

The booming mine camp's penchant for hard work and hard play also produced its share of "victimless" crime. Crap tables, roulette wheels, and back-room poker games were common at the 27 saloons that had cropped up by that time in the 1890s. An active red light district (there were 16 houses on "the row", stretching up Heber Avenue at the mouth of Deer Valley) produced the first of the town's memorable female characters.

Collectively termed "midnight angels", "fallen angels", or "ladies of the night", the women who worked in Park City's houses of prostitution were best known to the miners by fond nicknames such as Trixie, Frisco, and Copper Queen. Most enduring and famous among them was the 200-pound madam with a wooden leg known as Mother Urban. Noted for her generous contributions to charitable causes as well as her generous frame, Mother Urban was respected by both the girls who worked for her and town officials. She paid her fines without argument when the house was periodically raided by the sheriff's department. Mine officials realized they owed her a debt of gratitude for keeping the miners productive by keeping them entertained. Otherwise, they would have headed to Salt Lake City for their good times, and the long trip undoubtedly would have caused rampant absenteeism at the mines. The city treasury also was a beneficiary of prostitution, as monthly fines grew with the profession. In one typical month during 1899, the Justice of the Peace and Police collections amounted to $5 for assault, $30 for gambling fines, and $50 for prostitution fines.

The 1890s marked perhaps the most remarkable times in Park City's evolution from a frantic mine camp in the mountains to a wealthy community that attracted cunning investors from throughout the country. It was a time when both rags-to-riches and rich-to-richer stories abounded. The veins of silver, zinc, lead, and gold made millionaires of at least 23 common men and solidified the fortunes of those who arrived with money to invest. By 1896, when Utah attained statehood, the 7,000 residents of Park City had settled into a stratified society of the wealthy class and the working class.

The millionaires of the day became known as "the old Park City bunch." E.P. Ferry arrived from Michigan, where he owned a steamer line on Lake Michigan. Ample investment opportunities in Park City increased his fortunes. John Judge, a miner and later a mine foreman, amassed his fortune through slow but steady saving and investment, including the huge Alliance Tunnel that drained mining operations while providing the city's water. Miner and geologist David Keith arrived from Virginia City, Nevada, to supervise the installation of the giant 500-ton "Cornish pump", designed to remove water from the Ontario Mine. After bringing the pump to its working capacity of nearly four million gallons a day, Keith stayed on to amass his own millions in mining investments.

Three mines—the Ontario, the Anchor, and the Daly—dominated the town's fortunes as it moved toward the last decade of the Nineteenth Century. Clustered to the south of Park City, near the location of the first strike, they were surrounded by several other good, if lesser, producers with fanciful names such as Star of Utah, Little Bell, Constellation, and Nail Driver. But, men of vision and hope also were beginning to look toward Treasure Hill,

> Kearns' gilded-domed mansion in Salt Lake City included a bowling alley, billiard room, and ballroom, eventually became the official residence for Utah governors. In 1900, at age 38, Kearns was elected one of the youngest members ever of the U.S. Senate.

PARK CITY

defining Park City's western border, for possible new bonanzas. One such man was the legendary Thomas Kearns. Using a combination of hard work, intelligence, luck, and determination Kearns managed the transition from penniless to prosperous with such aplomb that he rarely was the subject of jealousy or gossip.

Legend has it that Kearns arrived on foot in Park City, in the late 1880s with only a pack on his back and ten cents in his pocket, stopping at Parley's Park to pitch hay in exchange for a meal. Irish in ancestry, Kearns was born in Canada and raised in Nebraska. His dreams of fortune began to take shape when he set off to prospect in the Black Hills of South Dakota at age 17. Later, he drifted south to Tombstone, Arizona, and eventually to Virginia City, Nevada, where he struck up a friendship with David Keith. Although he watched others make their fortunes with gold and silver strikes throughout the west, the fabled "glory hole" eluded Kearns for years. He was not discouraged enough to give up his search, however.

When Kearns first arrived in Utah, he took a job with the Denver and Rio Grande Railroad to save grub stake money. Then, with his pockets a bit fuller, he decided to leave Utah to try his luck in Montana. He had gotten as far as Idaho when he became fascinated with tales of the Park City discoveries. Ever an optimist, he set out to renew his friendship with David Keith. By that time, the Cornish pump had elevated Keith's reputation to near miracle-worker, and Keith was able to use his influence to help Kearns get a job at the Ontario Mine. Wielding a pick and shovel through the dark tunnels by day and studying geology at night, Kearns wasted no time in beginning his search for his own bonanza.

Keith's advice to Kearns was to go west—but only as far as the Woodside Ridge across the canyon from the Ontario and other large mines in production. Several strikes along the Woodside Ridge, on the slopes of Treasure Hill, already had begun to yield high-grade ore. Kearns began prospecting in earnest there. After looking at investment possibilities in several properties and digging unsuccessfully for new strikes, Kearns turned his attention to the Woodside Mine. He and Keith joined three other partners in a lease on the operation to dig a 200-foot tunnel. At the 170-foot level, they decided to run a drift and thoroughly explore the potential for lucrative veins in the area. Within days, they uncovered a huge ore vein that ran into the adjacent, undeveloped and seemingly unremarkable Mayflower claim. Almost immediately they began the serious business of forging partnerships, trading properties, amassing fortunes, and behaving like millionaires.

The first strike quickly earned the partnership $1.6 million. After various claims and ownership disputes were settled, Kearns and Keith found themselves in an unlikely, but lucrative, partnership arrangement with Albion Emery, a $3-a-day bookkeeper, wealthy investor John Judge, and W.V. Rice, secretary to mining mogul E.P. Ferry.

The outgoing Kearns immediately began earning the reputation of a leader, both in his business dealings and elsewhere. Stories circulated about his fondness for getting into the ring with professional boxers, even winning $1,000 when he beat a fighter named "The Terrible Turk" in Salt Lake City. His treatment of mining problems—such as disputes over underground tunneling into adjacent properties he didn't own—was forceful and direct. He always was ready to make a quick decision, close a deal, purchase what was necessary, and get on with the digging. Being a good Irish son, Kearns sent $20,000 to his parents in Nebraska from his first Mayflower earnings.

By following a vein from his Mayflower property into the nearby Silver King claims, Kearns began amassing the immense bonanza that would dominate Park City mining history for years to come. The Kearns partnership, impressed by the Silver King's vast potential, leased and then purchased the property. In less than a year, by August, 1892, they incorporated Silver King Mining Company for $3 million. Treasure Hill soon was underpinned with Silver King tunnels, including an upper level of three compartments sunk to 700 feet and a lower shaft reaching down to 1,000 feet. Dividends quickly rose to equal those of the famed Ontario mine on the other side of town.

Kearns' interests blossomed proportionately with his fortune, as he not only managed the Silver King, but actively involved himself in community issues. In 1892, he was elected to the Park City City Council; in 1894, he and David Keith served as Summit County representatives to Utah's Constitutional Convention.

Kearns also would soon become a social and political figure to be reckoned with well beyond Park City. Although his lovely Victorian mansion marked elegance in the mining community, it was eclipsed by his gilded-domed palatial home in Salt Lake City, just a block from

Heavy-handedness soon became R.C. Chambers' trademark. When he suspected the mining operation adjacent to the Ontario was taking ore from his mine, he had his men force out the neighboring miners by blasting tar and sulphur into their tunnels.

THE SILVER

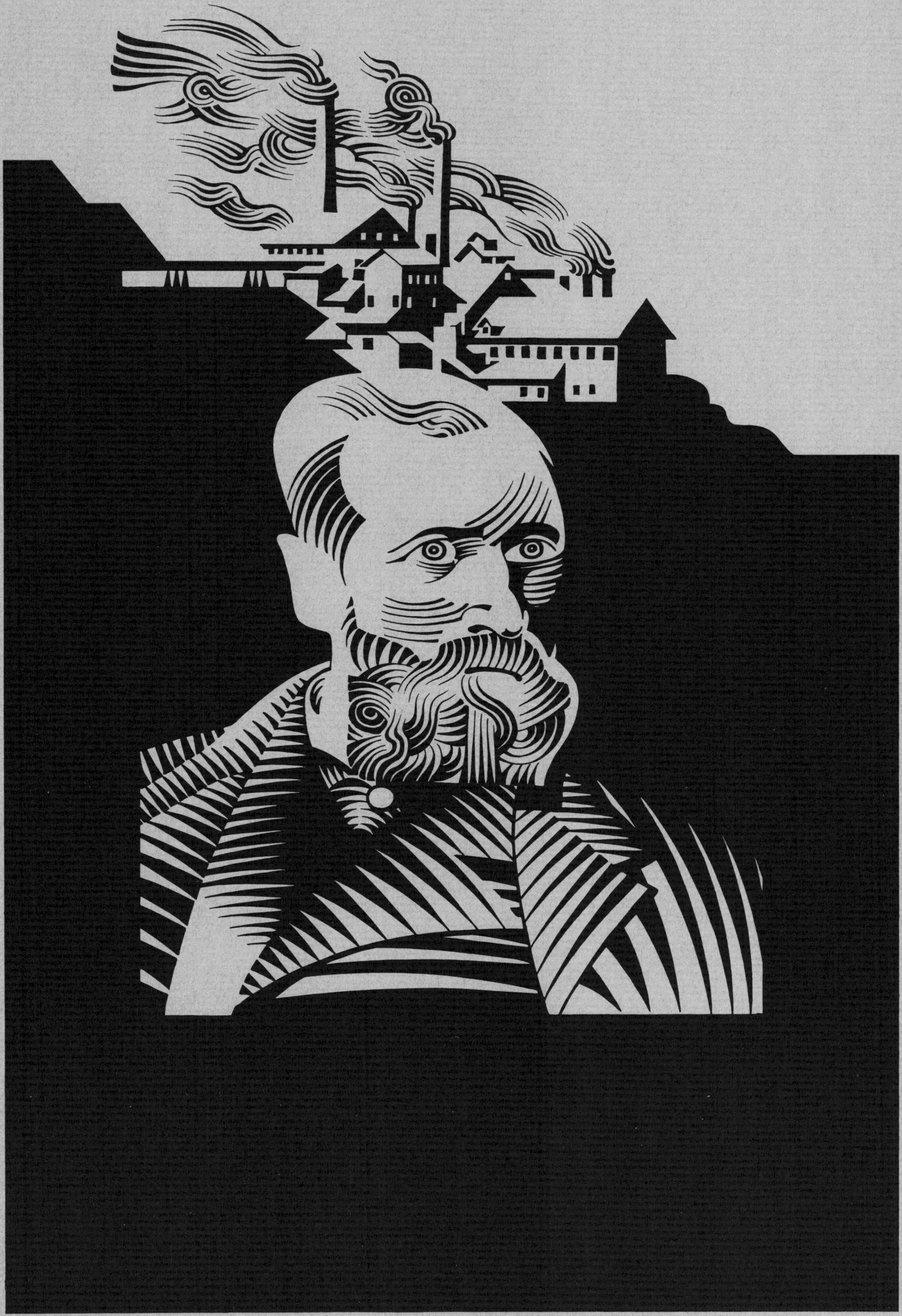

PARK CITY

> Plain folk had no love lost for Hearst's man, R.C. Chambers. They could not deny that his empire building for the Ontario made mining history and put Park City on the map.

THE SILVER

PARK CITY

the glass domed mansion built by David Keith. The 32-room Renaissance mansion, complete with bowling alley, billiard room, and ballroom, eventually became the official residence for Utah governors. The Kearns fortune also extended to the construction of the exclusive Alta Club in Salt Lake City, as well as two large downtown office buildings, the Kearns Building and the *Salt Lake Tribune* Building.

There seemed no end to Kearns' local and national interests. He and his wife Jennie, the niece of mining baron John Judge, donated large sums for construction of a Catholic cathedral in Salt Lake City. Later, they contributed $55,000 for the construction of St. Ann's Orphanage. In 1900, at 38, the portly prospector-turned-entrepreneur-turned-politician became one of the youngest men in history to be elected to the U.S. Senate. Although his one term was not marked by any particular achievement and he lost his bid for a second term, Senator Kearns did strike up a close friendship with President Theodore Roosevelt.

> Most enduring and famous among Park City's "Fallen Angels" was the 200-pound madam with a wooden leg known as Mother Urban. She was noted for her generous contributions to charitable causes as well as her chicken soup....

Kearns' saga of fortune and fame seems almost tame beside the whirlwind adventures of Susanna Bransford, the woman who became known as "Utah's Silver Queen." Born in 1859 to a pioneer family in Kentucky, Susanna crossed the plains to California with her parents. About 15 years later, she resettled in Park City, the town that would soon become responsible for her colossal fortune.

A hard working girl, variously employed as a seamstress and milliner, Susanna had more endearing charm than classic beauty. She found an appropriate match when at age 25 she married Albion Emery, a studious bookkeeper and later the Park City postmaster. Much to Susanna's good fortune, Emery turned a loan from R.C. Chambers into a quick bonanza as one of the original partners in the Silver King Mine; much to Al Emery's misfortune, however, overnight riches proved a bit too heady for Emery to handle. Although he became a Speaker of the Utah House of Representatives, he also established an inclination for alcohol that left him with a feeble heart and failing liver. He succumbed in 1894, just after returning from a vacation in Hawaii, leaving Susanna with a fistful of valuable mining stocks bonds and an eight-year-old adopted daughter.

It took all the business sense Susanna could muster, as well as a great deal of determination and patience, to turn Emery's interests into a working fortune. First, she had to defend a suit brought by the tenacious R.C. Chambers, who claimed that Emery's stock rightfully belonged to him due to the $8,000 he had loaned to start Emery's mining venture. Susanna held tough and eventually Chambers backed off, to much local surprise but little dismay. Thus, Susanna officially was launched as a mining entrepreneur. Through shrewd investments and a natural acumen for business, she soon had an income of more than $1,000 a day and was called "Utah's Silver Queen."

In 1899, during a business trip to Denver, Susanna was interviewed by a reporter from the *Denver Republican*. Her quotes had all the character of women's liberation well before its time: "I'm a business woman. Did you ever go down into a mine? It's awfully interesting. I go around from one to another to look after my affairs.... At first when they told me I must look after my business myself, it frightened me. But my lawyers laughed and said that's nonsense, so I just shut my eyes tight and went into it. I understand it now....

"I like to keep active. I'm the most impatient woman. Things must move around me.... I like to be independent and just go when and where I please.... I'm too busy to be a club woman. All the club women I know are women who have nothing else to do....

"I have only one fad—horses. I don't like dogs or any other pets, but I do love horses. I'm proud of my horses too."

The *Denver Republican* commented, "It's the most paradoxical thing to image that this pink and white creature, with big childish eyes and all fluffy in laces and ribbons, is a woman who manages a dozen or so mines so cleverly...."

Susanna later made another highly appropriate match for herself. She married Edwin Holmes, a lumber and mining millionaire from Chicago who was living in Salt Lake City while watching after his investments at Park City's Anchor Mine. Holmes shared Susanna's growing fondness for all things luxurious—big houses, sumptuous entertainment, yachting throughout the world, jewels, and furs. The wedding took place at New York City's Waldorf-Astoria Hotel. When the couple returned to Utah, Holmes purchased the famed Amelia Palace in Salt

THE LEGENDS

PARK CITY

Lake City, a Gothic mansion Brigham Young had built.

Twenty decorators from Marshall Field Department Store in Chicago bustled about the mansion, transforming it into a showcase appropriate for a Silver Queen. Gold leaf trim, Persian silk tapestries, silk brocade wallcovering, and international works of art complemented the lavish entertainments held at Amelia Palace. Salt Lake City was only one of their homes. Susanna also entertained political figures in Washington, D.C., and became a storied hostess in the newspapers of New York City. In Europe, she was welcomed to the chic Paris fashion collections and even danced with the Prince of Wales.

In 1924, Susanna and Edwin sold the palace to the Mormon Church and moved to Pasadena, California. (Amelia Palace was demolished in 1926, and a Federal Reserve Bank was built on the site.) After three years in California and 28 years of marriage, Holmes died, leaving Susanna a wealthy—this time phenomenally wealthy—widow once again. Susanna quickly set about healing her mourning wounds by undertaking a whirlwind travel schedule, checking in occasionally at one of the residences she maintained in New York, Pasadena, London, and Paris.

Although she was nearing 70, Susanna was ever charming and ever alert to the possibility of a new marriage. After all, her apt personal motto by now was the oft-repeated, "Why live if you can't enjoy yourself?" On one of her European trips, in 1930, she met and married a handsome Serbian physician, Radovan Nedelkov Delitch. This time, the match proved less than ideal; the doctor proved considerably less worldly and sophisticated than Susanna had thought. She divorced him within two years. Not long after, Delitch hanged himself in his cabin during a trans-Atlantic cruise.

Undaunted, Susanna wasted barely a year in capturing the fancy of the international rumor mill—this time as the female segment of a love triangle involving two Russian princes. By 1933, the triangle had shrunk to a duet, and Susanna married the official Russian Vice Counsel, Prince Nickolas Engalitcheff, a descendant of Ghengis Khan and heir of Russia's most prominent family. After civil and Russian Orthodox ceremonies in New York City, Susanna took the stately appellation "H.R.H. Princess Engalitcheff" and resumed her world travels.

That marriage also was short-lived, however, ending abruptly when the Prince died in 1935. By that time, Susanna, 76, had tired of her fast-paced life. She returned to Utah in 1938 for the first time in years, amid rumors that the young man who trailed behind as her business manager was in fact her latest love. However, she shunned suggestions that she was ready for remarriage with a terse, "I am unfortunate in keeping husbands."

She kept her word, and died a widow at age 83, quietly passing away while on a trip to visit friends in the East. By that time, her fortune had dwindled substantially, and there were only about 5,000 shares of mining stock left to leave to her business manager. True to the flamboyant "Silver Queen" notoriety, Susanna did not pass away without some rumor and speculation. As she was laid to rest beside Albion Emery in a Salt Lake City cemetery, there were whispers of possible suicide or even foul play. But then it would have been inappropriate for the Silver Queen legend to have ended with no fanfare.

The Gay Nineties were aptly named for Park City's fun and fortune set, those magnates and mavericks who were quick to become living evidence of a prediction once made by Abraham Lincoln: "Utah will become the treasure house of the nation." They adorned themselves for costume balls and frequented the lavish Grande Opera House, which was built with $30,000 in subscriptions from local residents. Or they called at Joe Dudler's popular new restaurant and saloon at the top of Main Street. They joined any of a number of well organized fraternal lodges, from the Ancient Order of the Hibernians to the Sons of St. George; and they wagered for high stakes at faro, roulette, and blackjack in the back rooms of local saloons.

For the more sports-minded gamblers, there were horse races in Deer Valley. In summers, winter-weary Parkites made excursions to Hot Pots in Heber Valley, just to the east of Park City. There they enjoyed leisure days of picnicking or taking the warm natural mineral baths. Or they could catch the Denver and Rio Grande train to Salt Lake City for a day of shopping.

The proliferation of retail establishments and businesses in Park City made trips to Salt Lake City less necessary as the 1890s moved toward the turn of the century. Stationery and newspapers were purchased at Woodruff Brothers, while Tim O'Keefe's offered an impressive line of cigars. Welsh, Driscoll and Buck seemed a forerunner of K-Mart, with clothing, heavy mine equipment, furniture, hardware, and even liquor. Children stopped in for sticky candy, while prospectors selected sticks of dynamite. Pioneer painter, poet, and photographer Willis A. Adams opened a photography shop and recorded much of Park City's early history. James Ivers ran a lively stable, while Kimball Brothers Stage expanded to include service to Brighton, just across the high pass to the south The Chinese still were noted for their laundries, the

THE LEGENDS

PARK CITY

> The local Judge, noting the difficulty in arresting frequent barroom brawler Bill Bennett, and the problems of keeping a law officer, appointed Bennett City Marshal.

THE LEGENDS

PARK CITY

Germans for their restaurants, and the Irish for their saloons. Scores of Park City establishments were listed in the San Francisco-published business guide, *Business Directory and Gazeteer*.

Like so much good news, there also was a bad news side to the heady flush of prosperity in those Park City salad days. The hundreds of wage-earning miners trudged to work in subzero temperatures and fought the chill of hip-deep water in the tunnels, never knowing when a sudden drop in silver prices might force a pay cut. The last thing on their minds was what to wear to the opening at the Opera House or the dance at Dudler Hall that night. Chinese cooks, Scandinavian loggers, and others whose earnings didn't include sudden silver bonanzas were plagued with worries about sickness that could sweep into their crude cabins with the winter winds and muddy spring thaws, spelling premature death for family members.

Thirty-four men were killed in the worst of several Park City mine disasters when a powder magazine exploded at the Daly-West mine. Avalanches and dynamiting accidents also took their tolls annually at the mines, but perhaps the most dreaded malady of all was the coughing, choking sickness known as "miner's consumption." More accurately termed silicosis, the painful lung disease was the natural result of breathing air filled with quartz dust from the underground drilling operations. Quartz particles, lodged in the soft lung tissues, eventually would open chronic wounds, and the fate of the stricken miner was almost always terminal. Even millionaire John Judge, who put down his pick and shovel after discovering his own bonanza, died of the dreaded miner's consumption.

It was appropriate, then, that the town's hospital, which was built in 1904, was called Miners Hospital, with the miners' new union, the Western Federation of Miners, spearheading a drive to raise money for its construction and furnishing. Miners had no monopoly on illness, of course. One of the early ordinances passed by City Council prescribed the required quarantine procedures and durations for cholera, smallpox, scarlet fever, bubonic plague, typhoid fever, spinal meningitis, and diptheria. Worried about sanitary conditions in Park City, the Council also passed an ordinance stating, "No cattle, horses, mules, swine, sheep, or goats shall be allowed to run at large in any street, lane, alley, road, or public grounds of this city."

Citizens also had to contend with the environmental problems engendered by growth in the mining industry. Giant clouds of smoke belched over the town from a growing number of mills and smelters, most noticeably the Marsac Mill just behind Main Street. The major creek flowing through town, originally known as Silver Creek for its sparkling waters and fine crop of mountain trout, eventually succumbed to toxic mine tailings and was renamed "Poison Creek." Smoke and fumes were such a common way of life in Park City, it's not surprising that those who could afford to—such as David Keith and Thomas Kearns—moved to more livable areas in and around Salt Lake City.

Dust swept up from Park City's unpaved streets during the dry summer season, stinging eyes and adding to the yellow haze spewing from the smelters. Noise pollution was another source of stress. Ninety-four times a minute, heavy iron rods called "stamps" slammed into the ore at Marsac Mill, crushing the rock with a deafening noise that reverberated throughout the mountains.

In 1901, with Silver King Mine dividends topping $1 million, the company began construction of an aerial tramway to replace the costly wagon hauling operation that brought ore to Treasure Hill. Eighty ore buckets swung along a mile-and-a-half long cable suspended from 40 towers. But, as usual, progress had its price: Noisy unloading took place near the center of town, and nearby property owners reported droppings from ore buckets in their yards.

Sam Raddon proved himself an early environmentalist, taking on the town's economic livelihood to speak out on pollution and health issues. In 1894, the *Park Record* said, "Half the town is usually without water and the streets are constantly

"Plumbob" Walker, self proclaimed local astrologer, used a carpenter's plumbob in his constant search for silver.

HARD TIMES

PARK CITY

being torn up to make repairs, to say nothing of water being furnished that would poison a hog, and many a life has been sacrificed through its agency—at least so the doctors affirm...The evil from which this camp has suffered since its foundation must be remedied."

Cleaning up Park City generally proved to be easier said than done. Few city officials did not have a close connection with the mines, and their sympathies often rested more with mining profits than citizen protests. Furthermore, cleanup had its costs, and the local one-enterprise economy often was just too precarious to support needed capital improvements. During 1893 and 1894, for example, hundreds of miners found themselves out of work when silver prices plummeted to less than 70 cents an ounce. The Anchor, Daly, Silver King, and other mines closed down for lack of profitability under the circumstances. Sheer determination and wage cuts kept some mines open, although many residents pulled up stakes and went prospecting elsewhere in the West.

Those who stayed saw silver prices improve and mines reopen in 1895 and 1896, although the fluctuations that began earlier had marked the start of a roller coaster existence for mining in Park City. In 1897, with the nation committing to the gold standard, silver prices dipped again, followed by more mine closings and wage cuts. Hope alternated with hopelessness, but the Spanish-American War forced silver prices up again in 1898, although several dozen of Park City's unemployed miners enlisted before they could enjoy the benefits of another economic upswing.

Up-and-down again silver prices did little to dampen the strike-it-rich dreams of miners.

Solon Spiro, was a German immigrant whose dream took shape in the form of a tunnel that could provide both a route to silver ore and drainage for water. He even scraped together financing to complete 15,000 feet of his tunnel, but the big bonanza eluded him. The money he did make was completely absorbed paying off debts.

A tall gangly miner, known affectionately as "John the Baptist" was a common enough sight roaming the dirt streets and mumbling religious pronouncements in his beard.

So on that fateful Saturday night in June, 1898, Park City already had been marked by an adventurous past and an optimistic future. Confusion still reigns as to how the fire started, but where it started was definitely and unfortunately in the center of town, at the American Hotel. A Chinese cook spotted the first flames leaping from the building, and, within minutes, Sheriff Thomas Walden fired three pistol shots to alert the sleeping town.

Local fire brigades rushed to the incinerating hotel, only to have their attempts set back as flames leapt over to the next building and the next along Main Street. Soon, the entire town took on a sickening orange glow as winds fanned the fire in every direction. Merchants and residents rushed from buildings with their most prized possessions, but the cause seemed lost before anyone could even put up a fight. Fire departments called in from Salt Lake City, Ogden, and Coalville could do little but dowse the flames that already had ravaged every structure in their path.

Homes in strategic locations were dynamited to put vacant lots in the fire's path and stop its spread. But the gallant effort did little to slow the fire's progress. To the east of Main Street, the shacks of Chinatown served as kindling to help fuel the flames. Once fueled, they continued upward until 75 homes on Rossi Hill were gutted. Both opera houses and City Hall on Main Street quickly were reduced to rubble, and the *Park Record* building went up like a torch. To the west, all of Park Avenue seemed alive with dancing flames, as the new Episcopal and Congregational churches, as well as dozens of residences, collapsed like match boxes.

After eight hours of exhausting fire fighting, the flames finally seemed to be contained—but a shocking 75 percent of Park City had been lost. The toll numbered hundreds of homes and business establishments, including most of Main Street, Chinatown, Rossi Hill, and Park Avenue. Five hotels were demolished, in addition to four churches, six restaurants, two banks, twelve saloons, and scores of other buildings. Miraculously, not a single human life was lost, although much livestock perished.

The community had two choices—abandon or start over. There was never any doubt that rebuilding was the popular option among men and women who had

HARD TIMES

PARK CITY

become well accustomed to braving hard times. Donations began pouring in to assist the shell of a town from individuals and business establishments from as far away as California. Salt Lake City Corporation sent $1,000; Evanston, Wyoming, sent $220; and Alma, Wyoming, sent $175. The Silver King Mine contributed $2,000. David Keith and Thomas Kearns each donated $500. Farmers and merchants from the Salt Lake Valley area sent railroad carloads of food and clothing, with the Denver and Rio Grande hauling relief supplies free of charge. The *Park Record*, which had lost its printing presses and valuable documents, moved its editorial offices to a tent and was printed by the *Salt Lake Herald*. The paper never missed an issue. Seeming almost as an omen of the situation, the *Park Record* had philosophized to readers a year earlier: "The darkest hours of night are those which immediately precede the dawn. Park City is now enveloped by the deepest darkness she has ever known; but the dawn is at hand…"

With the first mountain snows just a few months away, the scramble to reconstruct reached a fury during July and August. By the first of July, 25 of the devastated buildings either were reconstructed or under construction. And by late July, the Park Record could report that an average of one building per day was being completed. Unfortunately, there was little time to worry about quality, and much of what went up was the most slap-dash wooden construction. Still, several establishments opted for improvements. A substantial new brick-and-stone building was erected to house the offices of the Silver King Mine and the First National Bank. An elegant new theatre, named the Dewey in honor of Commodore George Dewey, replaced the Opera House. It boasted a 25-foot deep stage, a mechanical floor that tilted to accommodate either stage performances or ballroom dancing, and a bowling alley in the basement.

Unfortunately, Park City permanently lost some of its ethnic character to the flames that claimed homes and cottage industries in Chinatown. Many of the Chinese residents saw the fire as a bad omen and moved out of town when superstition got the better of them. The wide China Bridge crossing Rossi Hill never was restored to more than a narrow foot bridge, and only several dozen Chinese stayed to reconstruct their lives and homes.

The busy residents who did stay managed to reconstruct City Hall within months, as well as the post office, numerous business establishments, and several churches. The mining camp was a bustling place again.

The building boom continued into the Twentieth Century, as Park City grew in size and economic optimism. The handsome stone Washington School, the Jefferson School, the first Mormon Church (the "Blue Church"), and the Miners Hospital all were products of the era, along with a number of striking Victorian residences on Park Avenue and Woodside Avenue. The city government even added a baseball field to its properties.

The mining industry also was happily booming along through the early years of the new century, spurred by new strikes, new incorporations, and lucrative consolidations. The Daly-Judge Mine paid its first dividend: $112,000, in 1908. By 1912, the Silver King Mine had paid out $14 million in dividends. There even were a few new strike-it-rich stories. Sam Hair was a Heber Valley farmer who did a bit of hiking and exploring in the mountains whenever he had a chance. On one of these forays, he stumbled across an interesting rock outcropping that proved to be richly laced with silver and lead. His lucky strike became the Revelator Mine; the Revelator was not a giant of the industry, but it was more than adequate for one man's dreams of lasting fortune.

With silver prices alternately soaring and sagging as the Roaring Twenties drew near, the Federal government dealt Park City a blow when it passed Prohibition in 1917. Not only were lively Parkites to be denied a prime source of entertainment, but the *Park Record* estimated the town would lose a revenue source worth $22,000 annually.

On the last day of legal drinking, there hardly was a sober soul in the town. The saloons of Main Street became a beehive of excitement and revelry that lasted until midnight, as bartenders pushed to sell their last drop of booze and patrons stumbled behind the bars to grab any bottle they could carry home. The *Record* reported that as the final hour neared, "Empty barrels and empty ice cream freezers and everything else that would roll down the paved street were set in motion amid drunken yells and loud hurrays by the midnight revelers."

Prohibition, evidently didn't stop many determined

> Susanna Bransford possessed more endearing charm than classic beauty. Eventually….she was dubbed throughout her worldwide travels, "Utah's Silver Queen."

A NEW CENTURY

PARK CITY

> On the last day of legal drinking, there hardly was a sober soul in the town. The saloons of Main Street became a a beehive of excitement and revelry that lasted right up to midnight....

Park City drinkers. Periodic raids yielded ample bootleg liquor, as well as a pronunciation by federal agents that Park City was "the wettest spot in Utah."

In 1919, another government act had a more favorable response from the community. The Walsh-Pittman Act set the minimum price of silver at $1 an ounce, guaranteeing at least a specific level of security to mine investors and employees. The born-again mining boom in Park City meant the re-opening of smaller mines that had been closed for years.

With silver prices on the rise once again, Park City was able to partake in its share of the "roar" of the 1920s. As always, progress and prosperity could be tallied best by witnessing the construction of new buildings. The Orpheum Theatre brought entertainment within easy reach of residents in the lower Main Street area, although entertainment on upper Main Street suffered a setback when the roof of the Dewey Theatre collapsed from the weight of heavy snow. In its place, the more contemporary Egyptian Theatre was constructed in 1926. One of many Egyptian revival style buildings constructed during the excitement following the discovery of King Tut's Tomb, Park City's Egyptian boasted rows of giant pillars, replicas of Egyptian artifacts, a lotus blossom ceiling design, and exterior hieroglyphic tile motif.

During the 1920s, skiing enthusiasts also discovered the soft silver powder and wide variety of terrain in the hills around Park City. Trudging up the slopes, with leather shoes and long wooden boards, the early skiers had more fun than form as they slid back down with little opportunity to dig in an edge or carve a turn. The newly formed Utah Ski Club drew attention to the area when it chose Park City as the site of its annual meet in 1922. Ecker Hill, north of Snyderville, was a favored spot for ski jumpers, including the 1929 distance jumping record holder, Axel Andrason. Alf Engen set a world record at Ecker Hill the following year.

But even the most dedicated businessmen, community leaders, and sports enthusiasts could do little to survive the coming grim years. The good old days ended abruptly with the Crash of 1929. By 1930, silver had dropped to 38 cents an ounce; by 1931, to an unprecedented 25 cents an ounce. Mines cut wages, then announced layoffs, then closed down altogether.

Those who remained in the mine camp saw better times briefly again in 1933, but the economy of the town was shaky, at best, for the next 30 years. Fluctuating metal prices, labor strife, and increasing water problems in the mines seemed to defeat all hopes for a better future. For families that hung on, life was a quiet, constant struggle. By 1950, only 1,000 residents remained.

One of those families was the Hanley family, who worked a farm on the north end of town. Gerry Hanley, who was born in 1923 at the Miners Hospital, remembers his years growing up in Park City as, "A time when there just wasn't much to do at all. Most of the time, you could've shot a cannon down Main Street without hitting anyone."

As Park City slipped into a Rip Van Winkle sleep, it became known widely as a western mining ghost town—one of those places with a rich and lively past that would long be remembered...but never revived.

HANGING IN

PARK CITY

> Located at 7,000 feet in the rugged Wasatch Mountains, Park City is bordered by three world-class ski areas: Park City Ski Area, Deer Valley and Park West.

EAGLE'S VIEW

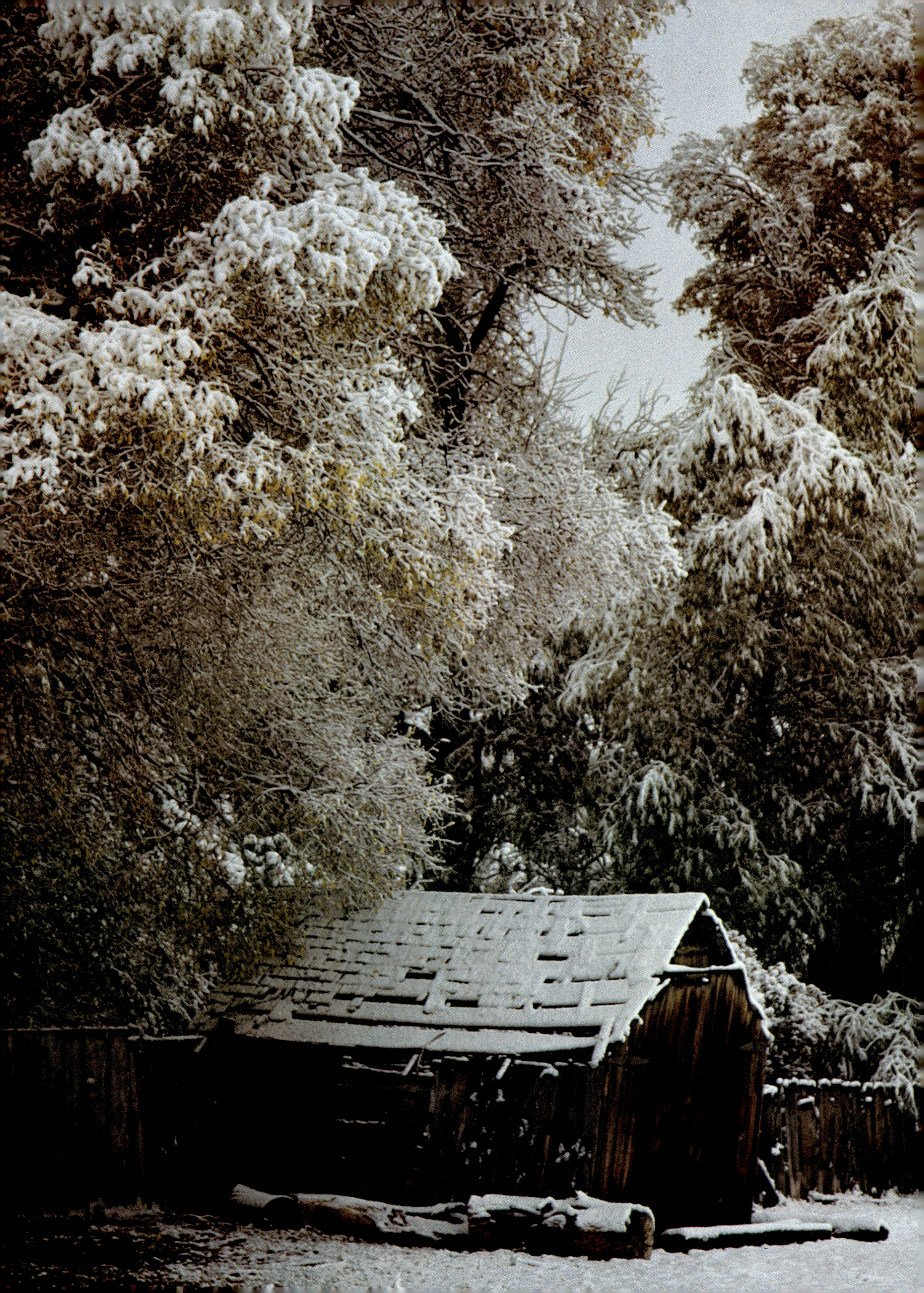

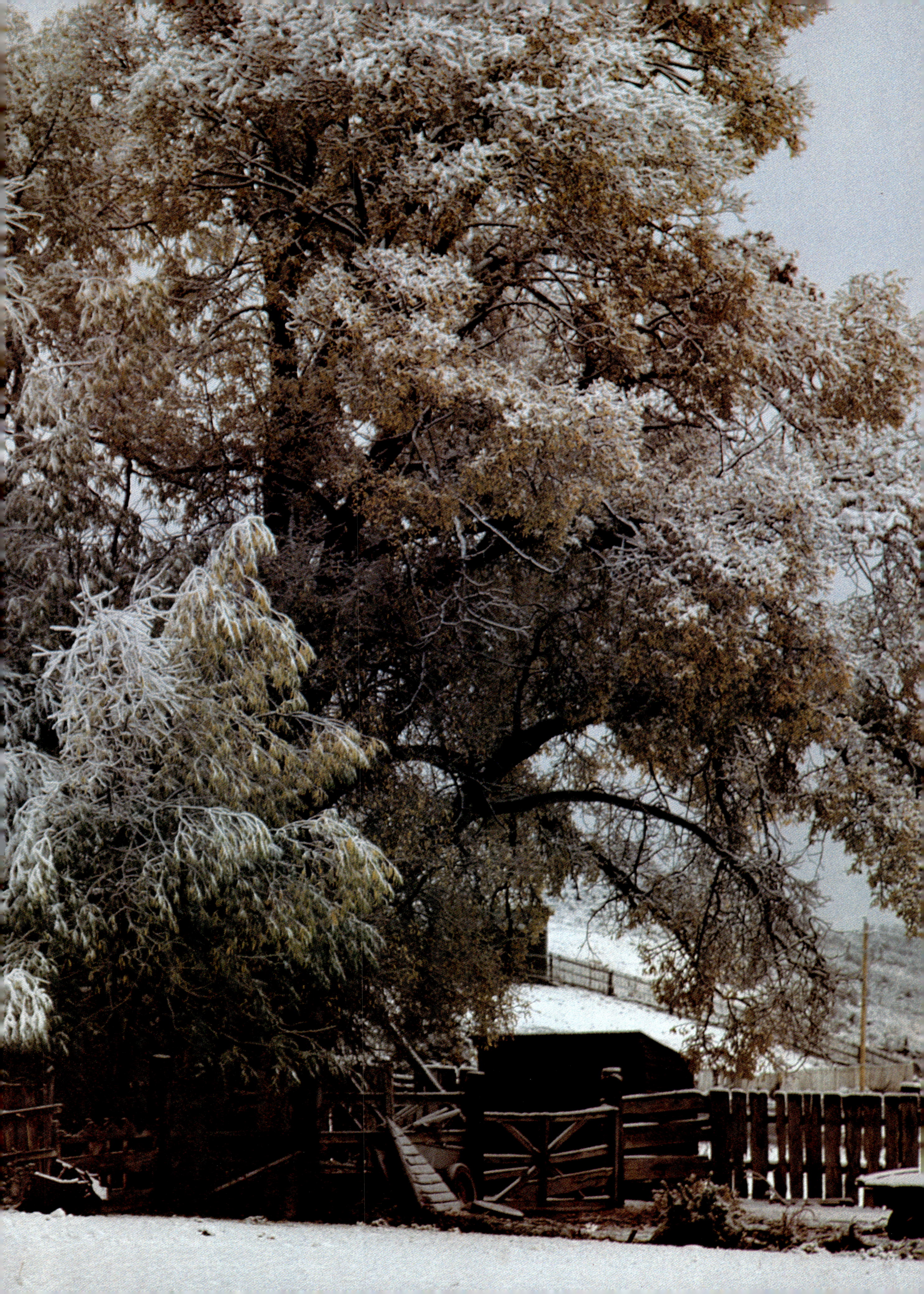

P A R K   C I T Y

S N O W   C O V E R

PARK CITY

Snow, the delight of skiers and the demon of motorists, blankets Park City from November to May, from Old Town to new suburbs.

SNOW COVER

P A R K   C I T Y

Park City's architectural heritage, sometimes restored, sometimes replicated, is a blend of numerous 19th and 20th century themes.

E V O L V I N G

PARK CITY

EVOLVING

PARK CITY

"Old Town," Park City's historic district, includes some remaining original structures and Victorian memories. Main Street is one of only a few business districts in the country to be named to the National Register of Historic Places.

BACKWARD FORWARD

PARK CITY

> "The miners, the ranchers,
> the cowboys....they're gone.
> They made big bucks
> and took them out of town.
>
> The builders, the bankers,
> the realtors....they're here.
> They bought the town
> with little money down."

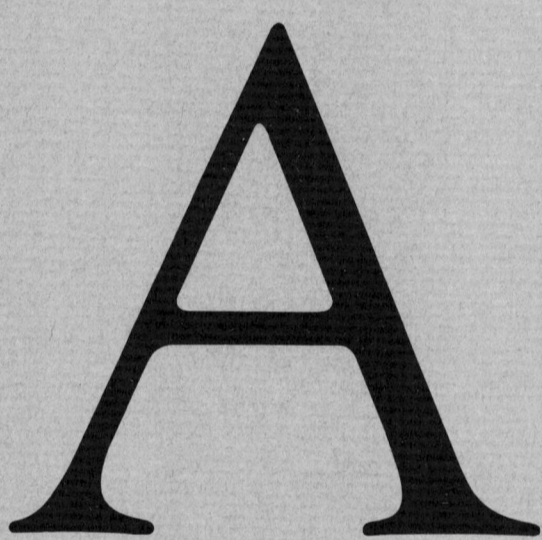

A refrain in the musical review, "This is the Place", written for the Park City centennial celebration, depicts the change—yes, progress—that occurred as Park City moved from mining boom town to ski resort. And, the evolution—especially during the runaway growth years of the 1970s and 1980s—has been accompanied by collective outcries that morn the passing of "the way it was."

The most serious of laments charge that the town has lost its "small town" character—its distinction as a place where everybody knew everybody, parking never was a problem, saloons were full of "locals", taxes hardly were worth a worry, and the scale of buildings was somewhat less than multi-storied and massive.

Ready to counter those charges are Parkites—many of them old-timers—who note that many of the original, now demolished, buildings weren't really worth preserving anyway, and the newer additions are neater, cleaner, and more functional. Additionally, numerous proponents of a changed Park City point to improved city services and such amenities as tennis courts, ski lifts, golf courses, movie theatres, a supermarket, and a variety of retail shops.

The debate about present and future successes and mistakes undoubtedly will continue for years to come. However, a few things remain constant: the clean air, awesome mountain scenery, silver snow, shimmering aspens, and significant heritage—and, of course, the eclectic group of individuals who call Park City home...

UPDATE

PARK CITY

A few stalwart residents who hung on through Park City's sleepy years during the 1940s and 1950s, had faith in the town's future. They believed that reports of the town's death were premature. After all, Bessie Wheeler still was managing the purple painted "parlor" that in 1956 became the town's last house of prostitution to close down. The Park City High School band still was consistently winning top honors in state competitions and in 1950 was chosen as the featured band for halftime entertainment at the Shriners East-West All Star Football Game in San Francisco. Some Main Street saloons and restaurants still operated through the 1940s, as did the Park Hotel and Frankel's Clothing Store. The Ford Garage offered the latest models for the growing post-war family.

Otto Carpenter and Bob Burns were two of the most optimistic—and certainly foresighted—local entrepreneurs of the period. In 1946, they constructed Park City's first ski lift, a chair running 1,400 feet on pine poles. Called Snow Park, the infant ski area was located among tall firs and aspens in scenic Deer Valley. The "lodge" was a warmup hut where Carpenter's wife LaRue served coffee and hamburgers. Snow Park was not exactly a "destination resort," but it did attract good numbers of Salt Lake City and Park City area skiers. A Snow Park Ski Club was formed, lessons were offered, and carnivals and races made for exciting weekend sports entertainment.

Unfortunately, not everyone was as bullish on Park City. In 1946, the Denver and Rio Grande Railroad gave up its Parley's Canyon route, bringing an end to more than 50 years of railroad service to the town. When the union contract between mine workers and the Park City mines expired in 1949, it was not renewed. The mine closings put 800 mine and mill employees out of work. Doctors and dentists left town, and there wasn't even a barber left by the mid-1950s.

Ask any local who managed to hang in. The 1950s collectively are recalled as a dark period marked by deterioration, abandoned buildings, and ghosts. Signs over the doors of shops, businesses, and clubs came down, and boards went up on windows all over town. Already noted as a western ghost town in numerous books and legends, Park City quickly was catching up to its reputation.

Art Durante, who kept his family's popular Main Street hardware business going, later recalled, "The town was mostly boarded up.... There was only one grocery store on Main Street, called Earl's." Durante served on the City Council from 1948 to 1952. "The problems weren't so different then," Durante said later. "We still had to worry about streets being paved and snow being removed and all, but we managed on a lot less. The city budget for the whole year in 1948 was just $52,000."

Ken Kummer, who was born in Park City and worked in the mines, recalled that during the 1950s, "The town was just about done. The mines had closed and there wasn't much left to do but move houses for folks who would buy them and move them to other towns."

The handwriting was on the wall for United Park City Mines Company, the giant firm that had merged nearly all the area mines. Slumping domestic ore prices, combined with competition from imported ore and high production costs, convinced mining officials that there was little or no future in the area's underground tunnels. Recreation on the above-ground holdings was a possibility only if the financing could be found to make it happen.

That possibility moved closer to reality in 1961, when United Park City Mines vice-president and general manager Seth K. (Red) Droubay determined to apply for funds available to depressed areas through the U.S. Department of Commerce. UPCM board member Clark Wilson, in Washington, D.C., lobbying for controls on lead and zinc imports, stopped in on officials at the Commerce Department's Area Redevelopment Administration. Estimating that as many as 1,700 jobs could be created in Utah from the development of what was originally to be called "Alpine Treasureland" resort, the Commerce Department granted a $1.23 million loan. With matching funds from United Park City Mines, American Smelting and Refining Company, and Anaconda Company,

Bea Kummer donned an ankle-length black-and-white striped dress and broad-brimmed matching hat to conduct her "Main Street Walking Tours"...an educational glimpse of the original old mining town.

BOARDED UP

PARK CITY

construction began at the site of the present Park City Ski Area during the summer of 1962.

The initial funds were earmarked for construction of the longest aerial tramway in North America, a chair lift and two J-bars. They also provided for development of a base lodge and nine-hole golf course at the bottom of the slopes, while a Summit House at the 9,300-foot level crowned the top of the 10,000-acre resort and provided awesome views into Heber Valley and beyond. On May 11, 1963, Utah Governor George D. Clyde wielded the silver plated pick that broke ground for the new Park City project. After a summer and fall of frantic construction, on December 21, 1963, Park City Mayor William Sullivan cut the traditional ribbon to officially launch the two-and-one-half-mile gondola and open the Treasure Mountain Recreation Center. United Park City Mines president John Wallace drove the first ball down the fairway of the Treasure Mountain Golf Course 10 months later.

Almost overnight, activity became a new way of life in Park City. Those few residents still left grabbed paint brushes and pruning shears to spruce up their homes. Slowly, but surely, businesses that remained on Main Street began to remodel. A few boarded-up places even began to reopen. In the absence of any tough ordinances about signs or historic character, some of the new effort seemed to contribute to a hodge-podge of results. The classic and elegant 1926 Egyptian Theatre was remodeled in a frontier motif and named The Silver Wheel. But, the old-fashioned melodramas that played there proved to be the delight of both residents and visitors. Across Main Street, construction began on a huge box-like building, the 58-unit Treasure Mountain Inn condominium project. Although it eventually would be viewed as an unwieldy structure, truly uncharacteristic of the town's past or future, it did signal the community's long-term commitment to growth as a tourist and recreation area. A Wyoming couple purchased and reopened the New Park Hotel (now the Claimjumper) at the base of Main Street, while additional lodging—the Chateau Apres, the C'est Bon, and the Silver King—sprang up near the new Park City Ski Area.

Did all the town's "old timers" embrace and welcome the sudden growth and development? For the most part, they just didn't know exactly what to make of it. As Gerry Hanley recalled: "I remember the early planning meetings when projections of cars and skiers were made. None of us really believed it. We just thought we'd see a few big hotels at the base of a ski area on the north end of town. We never thought it would mean development all over town."

Not even the physical development made the most notable difference. Beyond the cranes and construction, beyond the new footings and facades, there also were new people. Salt Lake City residents began to venture up the canyon for skiing, to escape the summer heat, or just to have a good time in another environment. A few pioneers from other parts of the country even began to move in and call Park City home — if not for good, at least for the duration of one or two good ski seasons. If it was not the best of times, neither was it the worst of times. Growth had begun.

> John Price, the new mayor... had created a million-dollar business in surfboard manufacturing, starting with three employees and expanding to more than 100.

Harry Reed was typical of young men and women who were attracted by the excellent snow and opportunities to work and ski in the same place. Born in New York and raised in Delaware, Reed arrived in Salt Lake City as a 20-year-old college student to work a summer job with Hercules, Inc. It didn't take him long to notice the good times to be had up in the mountains. By 1964, he had moved up the canyon to Park City, rented a ramshackle house for $25 a month and begun working on the initial ski patrol at the new resort. His ski patrol colleagues were typical of the new mix of people in Park City. Several, such as Ron Smith, were from Salt Lake City; a few, such as Pete Toly, were Park City locals; some hailed from elsewhere, most of them from California.

"The town still was mostly boarded", Reed said. "In 1963 and 1964, there still were mainly locals living here and maybe about a half dozen or so of us ski bums from out of town—all guys. Ski bum girls came later. It was almost impossible to find a place to live, since residents were actually residing in their own homes back then, or else the abandoned homes were in no condition to rent."

Reed notes that he eventually bought a rickety old house on Main Street out of necessity. "Luckily, it was still possible to save a little money and buy a tumble-down place cheap to at least get a roof over your head....I remember Bill Coleman and his wife arrived from the Midwest and lived in their mobile home for a long time before they finally bought a small house for a few thousand dollars."

SKI BOOM

PARK CITY

Ed Brennan established one of Park City's most unusual living situations when he left his Aspen, Colorado, retail business, "Ed's Beds", to move to Utah. Somewhat of a Renaissance man and decidedly an individualist, he was a Yale graduate who wrote children's books. He arrived in Park City in an old bread truck, which he lived in with his dog, "Betty the Flea". For electricity, he simply uncoiled a long extension cord and hooked up to the ski resort supply.

Dale Nelson beat the housing problem by making a name—and a number of residences—for himself in buying and fixing up rundown houses. The first residence he bought in Park City in 1964 was typical of local housing stock at the time: It had no roof, no windows, and no doors. Nelson worked as a salesman for Mattel Toys, but he continued to acquire and renovate similar structures, soon owning six rental properties, including the Imperial Hotel and Antique Shop on upper Main Street. Nelson had gotten his first look at Park City in the 1950s when his family came on Sunday drives from Salt Lake City to look at the old ghost town.

Harry Reed notes there was little in the way of city services, then: "Just one old truck that was the sum total of trash collection. And you had to go to Salt Lake City for so many things—especially in the summers, which were dead up here. There were no pools and no tennis courts. It was real sleepy."

Bars were the primary source of Park City entertainment in the early 1960s, and everybody who remembers seems to agree that those days were the very best ever for the town's drinking establishments. "You just can't believe how many really good bars there were", Reed recalls. "And you had much more live entertainment to choose from than ever since." The live entertainment was, in fact, *very* lively. Go-go girls danced through the night at several clubs, and Shirley Price was the popular stripper at the C'est Bon, a jumping restaurant and bar with a night club that could seat several hundred people. The Red Banjo, the Silver Palace, the Forge, and other spots entertained large contingents from Salt Lake City who found the bars closing later and offering a greater variety of dance music and entertainment than was available down in the valley.

Mary Lehmer, whose family had a sheep ranch just north of town and lived part-time in Salt Lake City and part-time in Park City, recalled: "When the resort first opened, there was more activity here than Park City's ever seen since. Every other door was the swinging door of a bar or a restaurant, and people really knew how to have fun.... At the Oak Saloon, a beer cost you ten cents, water set-ups were free, and your third round was on the house. You also could bring your baby or toddler and let them play around the place while you were at the bar.... Dancing and drinking spilled right out onto the streets on weekend nights. Then, we'd all get together at Pop Jenks Cafe the next day and nurse our headaches and our hangovers over coffee and soft drinks."

Harry Reed remembers looking up at a line of skiers he was instructing to see one of his ski patrol buddies gliding behind the students with his ski pants around his ankles; Mary Lehmer remembers wondering if a bar would cash her check, to which the bartender replied, "Hell, yes. I'd cash it if you wrote it on a watermelon rind!" In those days, local bars had lavish floats in the Labor Day parades and tossed coupons for free beers into the crowds. Also, private clubs weren't so private that they'd actually insist on seeing a membership card.

Organized sports events also began to take place. In 1965, the annual Lowell Thomas Classic ski races were launched, complete with celebrities of the slopes such as Billy Kidd, Jean Saubert, and Jimmy Huega. Dog sled races were begun in earnest at Flinders Mountain Meadow Ranch, just down the road in Snyderville, and the Utah Snowmobile Association began holding meets in Park City.

One of the most memorable annual events for Salt Lake City visitors was the "Snowball Express", a train well-stocked with booze and good cheer that made its way each winter from Salt Lake City to Park City with as many as 500 revelers aboard. "It was a complete party on wheels", Mary Lehmer recalls. "You could do some serious skiing during the afternoon in Park City, but mostly you just drank and partied." Sponsored by the Salt Lake Area Chamber of Commerce, the "Express" made its popular annual run well into the 1970s.

The initial fun, frolic, and good fortune sparked by the opening of the ski resort turned out to be extremely short lived, however. According to the *Park City Coalition*, a small newspaper then in competition with the *Park Record*, "The mining company first opened the lifts in 1963 and 1964. These were pretty good years as Park City was new and kind of a novelty. However, the novelty soon wore off, and so did business."

Edgar Stern began eyeing Park City property in 1968, first considering purchase of some land at the base of the Park City Ski Area. But his vision expanded rapidly...

SKI BOOM

PARK CITY

A number of factors combined to put a damper on the first swell of activity that followed the excitement of becoming "a resort town." First, there was substantial difficulty in increasing the tourist market much beyond Salt Lake City; United Park City Mines was not in a financial position to further increase lodging and move toward a destination resort concept. Then, two things happened to dry up the Salt Lake City market. The highway up Parley's Canyon closed for several years to undergo major reconstruction and expansion, with traffic re-routed through a long and tortuous road up Emigration Canyon. Additionally, law enforcement entities began taking a harder stance concerning the control of liquor in Park City, cracking down on nearly everything— from the hours the bars stayed open to the way they regulated club memberships.

"It was ridiculous," Mary Lehmer recalled. "You could be having a nice evening at the C'est Bon, and suddenly there were guys in uniforms shining flashlights throughout the place." Added Harry Reed, "All of a sudden, the police were cracking down on everything. There were raids, arrests, and forced bar closings just at a time when some people were starting to be able to make a living here again....Well, Park City has never been exactly loved by the rest of the county or the rest of the state."

Park City's comeback seemed to fizzle, and the 1960s were ending with dampened promises. Expansion during that period largely was concentrated out of town. Summit Park opened as a residential community with homes tucked into pine-covered slopes and within reach of both Park City and Salt Lake City. A large ranch between Park City and Snyderville was sold to a California company that had plans for another major ski complex, Park City West, which eventually became Park West. The neighboring resort opened in 1968 with base facilities and three double chairlifts. As for Park City proper, the skiing still was excellent, but the town was no longer full of the dining and drinking set from Salt Lake City that once had filled it to capacity every weekend.

In 1969, the United Park City Mines Company began negotiating with Royal Street Development Company, Inc., about the sale of the ski resort. Royal Street chairman Edgar Stern and president Warren King had witnessed some successful development in Colorado and were ready to invest in the next good ski resort opportunity. In fact, Stern had been a driving force behind the development of the Aspen Institute and Aspen Music Festival, as well as numerous real estate dealings in the Colorado resort. He also had founded hotels in New Orleans and San Francisco and started the first television station in New Orleans. Stern's grandfather was the co-founder of Sears, Roebuck and Company.

So it was with the eye of a very successful, very creative entrepreneur that Edgar Stern began eyeing Park City property in 1968, first considering purchase of some land at the base of the Park City Ski Area. This vision expanded rapidly, however, and he soon was telling himself, "Let's not try to buy that little piece of land; let's try to put something together to buy the whole thing."

In April, 1970, United Park City Mines granted Royal Street a purchase option for its recreational facilities. The deal also included long-term leases on property in Deer Valley, and the Greater Park City Company was formed to reflect the joint venture interests of Royal Street and the mine company.

To characterize the Greater Park City Company as aggressive in its development program for Park City would be an understatement. The land buying and building that began in the early 1970s was the start of a divisive dilemma that Park City has suffered ever since: How much to grow? How fast? How tall? How dense? How contemporary? In 1971 and 1972, construction in the area of the ski resort and the golf course was frantic. Condominiums were the order of the day, with several hundred units dashed into place in barely a one-year period, all sporting pseudo-mining names or other lofty designations such as "Park Avenue," "Three Kings," "Crescent Ridge," and "Payday." To house reservations, sales, management, and maintenance, a large red barn-like structure was erected that echoed the old Silver King Coalition Mine building further up Park Avenue.

Up on the mountain, development was equally fast and furious. Miles of additional runs were cut to open new canyons to skiing, and new chairlifts were installed to accommodate the growing numbers of weekend and

> Determined to make the Deer Valley ski area a high luxury experience for all who visited, Royal Street spent $20 million before the first lift opened.

SKI BOOM

P A R K C I T Y

Stein Eriksen...
arrived from
stints with ski
resorts in Michigan, California,
and Vermont.
Necks craned
from chairlifts
to glimpse the
unmistakable
motion as Stein
carved and
cruised his way
down a slope.

S K I B O O M

PARK CITY

destination skiers. The United States Ski Team chose Park City as its headquarters in 1973, using the old Silver King Mine boarding houses midway up the mountain to house athletes during training.

To the particular delight of ski competition fans, Olympian Stein Eriksen came to Park City as director of skiing. The Norwegian who had captured gold and silver medals in the 1952 Olympics, as well as two golds in the 1954 World Ski Championships, arrived from stints with ski resorts in Boyne Mountain, Michigan, Heavenly Valley, California, and Sugarbush Valley, Vermont.

The new life that was breathed into the ski resort also brought a new influx of individuals. Many of them came to work for Royal Street itself. Bob Wells, Royal Street's vice-president, later was elected to City Council and began his own successful development firm. Jan Wilking arrived in 1970 to work in Royal Street's design department, but eventually became the publisher of the *Park Record*. Royal Street engineer Jack Johnson later opened the largest engineering firm in the area.

Even some people who had left town began returning. For example, Harry Reed had left his ski patrol career and the Park City slopes in 1966, but returned in 1970. He started a property management company and real estate firm in 1972, eventually becoming one of the most successful and respected real estate investors in town.

Some locals who had moved away during the lean years also heeded the call of a town on the boom again. Notable among these was Lloyd Stevens, who had been born in Park City and grown up on a farm in nearby Oakley. After service as a missionary in New Zealand, he worked as an architectural hardware consultant in Salt Lake City for awhile, then moved to Borrego Springs, California.

It was in California that Stevens began his restaurant career—the hard way. He lived across the street from the Red Barron Steak House. One evening the manager, desperate for help, came over to ask if anyone knew how to cook a steak. Stevens volunteered to help and he soon ended up managing the place. On a trip back to Utah, he noticed a distinct change in level of activity. "My dad said I ought to take a look at Park City, because this Royal Street Company was coming in and spending a lot of development money there."

By 1971, Stevens had leased the basement of the New Park Hotel to start a steakhouse on Main Street, the Claimjumper. "After the first year, we were $17,000 in debt, but by the next ski season we knuckled down and made money," he said. In 1973, he took on a partner and bought the entire building, expanding the Claimjumper to a hotel, restaurant, and club—one of the few such establishments in Park City that seems to continually flourish through varied ski seasons and fickle local preferences. "It was a good time to get a place off the ground," Stevens said. "There were a lot of fun places in Park City, and people were looking for fun things to do. Now it's harder, especially with the way the liquor laws are. It's tough to get really good entertainment, and people don't seem to go out to dance anymore. They go to big concerts now instead."

It also was a time when Park City seemed to attract a particularly eclectic mix of exotic and interesting individuals—all of whom seemed to acquire names to match. A guy soon known as "Steakhouse" (Jamie Gunzell) had arrived with Stevens to start the Claimjumper. Another well-known figure was "Waterbed" (Ron Purdom), who arrived from Hawaii and opened a waterbed store. When that market dried up, he went into partnership with "Strawberry" (Craig Masters), formerly of Mobil Oil Company, to start Mountain Realty real estate firm. "The Chief" (Darrell La Franier) strutted through town with a bandolier full of mini-bottles strapped from shoulder to waist and leather holsters on his hips cradling fifths of vodka.

Mary Lehmer, who had been commuting to Park City from Salt Lake City, moved to Park City full-time in 1970. An attorney, she had a successful practice in Salt Lake City, was appointed City Attorney in Park City in 1968, and she wasted no time in becoming a controversial, outspoken figure. In 1970, she was removed from her city attorney post in a feud over the administration of water and sewer rates. "We badly needed to equalize the rates, especially to see that businesses and lodges paid their fair share," Lehmer explained. "I went around and counted every pot in town, and then I sent every business person a letter about their new rates. Well, needless to say, they got up in arms over the whole thing."

Never one simply to slink away, Lehmer got into politics and won a term on City Council in 1972. In those times of fast growth and controversy about how to deal with it, politics in Park City were heated, to say the least. Lehmer can recall plenty of shouting, and even a fist fight incident during City Council deliberations. In one highly

NEW FACES

PARK CITY

unusual move, the Council ousted the entire Planning Commission when that body refused to grant a conditional use permit for nightly rental of Snow Country Apartments. Then the Council overturned the decision to deny the rental use permit.

"Of course, as always, our biggest problem was still what to do about dogs", Lehmer recalled. "This town was just laden with dogs running free all over the place."

Lehmer was particularly outspoken about the Greater Park City Company, which many long-time locals saw as taking over and running things its own way. The worry became especially acute in 1973 when, for the first time, a relative newcomer was elected mayor and another was elected to City Council. John Price, the new mayor, had arrived in Park City from Encinitas, California, in 1969. When he was still in his 20s in California, he had created a million-dollar business in surfboard manufacturing, starting with three employees and expanding to more than 100 within five years. By the time he moved to Park City, he was in a position to relax, enjoy the mountain sports, renovate older homes, and invest in real estate. With the support of a newly formed political action group called "Citizens for Productive Government", the 32-year-old Price was elected mayor. Another newcomer, Jan Wilking, won a seat on the Council.

With an old/new split in the city government, every issue seemed to be defined as the interests of Greater Park City Company vs. the old timers. Many of these were played out in public sniping between Councilwoman Lehmer and Mayor Price about what the resort company would or wouldn't be permitted to do. Price finally resigned in 1974, citing as a reason, "the underhanded and illegal methods employed by the Park City Council." In a parting shot, reported in an interview in the *Park City Coalition* newspaper, Price said, "My experience with Greater Park City Company is that they're the only honest people we have dealt with. It's the city that doesn't stick to its word. Mary has acquired a personal hatred for Warren King and the Company. It's obvious she's not voting in the public interest, she's voting against Greater Park City Company....I recommend....that Jan Wilking be appointed Mayor in that he is the only council member who knows Robert's Rules of Order..."

In fact, the next mayor of Park City was long-time resident Leon Uriarte, followed by two terms of another long time Parkite, retired postmaster Jack Green. "Sure I was outspoken", Lehmer says. "I was surrounded by people who wanted to give this town away to developers. And it wasn't just the resort; our own locals were pretty quick to sell us out when they saw ways the Company interest could benefit their own personal interest."

When the 1975 City Council campaign rolled around, Lehmer did not file as a candidate for a second term. She did garner a good portion of write-in votes, although not enough for re-election.

That year also produced one of the more bizarre and good humored candidacies in Park City election history. A young resident named O.D. McGee ran for City Council on what he termed the "graft and corruption platform." His tongue-in-cheek campaign slogan referred to him as: "O.D. McGee—Your Fun Candidate." In a newspaper interview, McGee made his ironic charge:

"The most important issue facing Park City is the dog issue. I would like to at least double the dog population. We are going to bus underprivileged and impoverished dogs from neighboring communities using City funds.... There simply aren't enough dogs in Park City.... Basically, I'm conducting my campaign by kissing babies and shaking hands."

Although he received only 20 votes, O.D. McGee at least gave the electorate a topic of conversation beyond the grim debate about how Park City could survive its own rapid expansion and development.

The recession of 1974 slowed growth in Park City somewhat, and was particularly unkind to both the Park City Resort and Park West. The latter was purchased at foreclosure by Californians Jack Roberts and Harold Babcock, who immediately began an expansion program to make the smaller ski area competitive and prosperous. Royal Street sold the

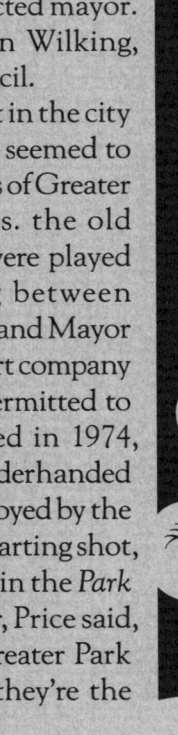

> Lloyd Stevens began his restaurant career the hard way....the manager, desperate for help, asked if anyone knew how to cook a steak. Stevens volunteered to help and soon ended up managing the place.

NEW FACES

PARK CITY

Park City Resort to Alpine Meadows of Tahoe, Inc., headed by Nick Badami, who knew how to make a ski area flourish. The resort soon sported new runs and lifts and an expansive expert area, Jupiter Bowl.

Royal Street was not doing as well with its other properties. The Park Avenue condominiums were selling so poorly that a cut-rate sale was the only recourse left. The asking price for a unit was slashed in half, and the sale was heavily marketed in Salt Lake City. Dozens of condominiums were snatched up in a few days. The event initiated a renewed interest in Park City among many Salt Lake City residents, sparking an incredible upsurge in Park City development. So incredible, in fact, that by 1979 the valuation of new construction reached a record $8 million, then soared to $74 million two years later. With the year-round population growing slowly and leveling off at about 4,000, it was apparent that Park City's future would be in second homes owned by non-residents.

Growth was the continual good news/bad news story of the 1970s. While it brought noise, traffic, and some dense and bulky physical structures to the once quaint and sleepy town, it also brought economic energy, a tax base that could support increased city services, and an interest in community activities and cultural events. It also brought tourists, of course. Local historian and newspaper columnist Bea Kummer donned an ankle-length black-and-white-striped dress and broad-brimmed matching hat to conduct her Main Street Walking Tours, an educational walk down Main Street for a last glimpse at what still could be seen of the original old mining town.

Among the first indications that summer really would reach the status of one of the four seasons in Park City — albeit a very short season — were the development of a rugby team and the founding of an annual arts festival, both of which were launched in the summer of 1970. The 1970 rugby season actually consisted of only two games for the unconditioned and untrained Park City team.

The next year was another matter, however, with the Park City Muckers posting some impressive wins and initiating the first Annual Park City Rugby Challenge Cup, an event marked by parties, barbeques, drinking contests…and even rugby games.

Visiting teams in the Park City Rugby Challenge have included players from California, Colorado, New Mexico, Virginia, and elsewhere in the United States, in addition to the South Pacific island of Tonga (largely by way of Brigham Young University) and Australia (largely by way of a destroyer docked in San Francisco).

The development of the Park City Arts Festival generally is credited to Jim Patterson and Mike Dontje. They liked the idea of turning over Main Street to the arts for a weekend. Local artists and merchants rose to the occasion, and, somewhat to the astonishment of its founders, the first Festival in 1970 drew 7,500 attendees.

Since then, the Festival has taken over the town for a weekend each August, attracting annual crowds estimated at more than 100,000. Sponsorship passed on to the Park City Chamber of Commerce and then to the Kimball Art Center; the activities grew to include live music, stage performances, and dance.

Park City arts got a permanent home with the opening of the Kimball Art Center in 1976. William Kimball visited Park City from his home in San Francisco in 1975 and quickly became enamored with both the town and the idea of a local art center. Searching for a likely structure for the proposed center, he checked out the Blue Church Lodge on Park Avenue and the old Masonic Building on Main Street, then settled on the abandoned Eley Garage at the base of Main Street. It was large, ugly, and in need of a complete interior gutting and new facade. But, by November, 1976, it had been transformed into the space to house a large exhibit gallery, workshops, a gallery shop, and places for classes and performing arts.

"Clown Day" quickly grew beyond clowns and beyond the ski area, with a Halloween atmosphere permeating the town from Alpha Beta to Main Street.

GROWING PAINS

PARK CITY

> Tina Lewis got the idea that the old, boarded-up Miners Hospital might make an ideal home for a new city library. When it opened, more than 700 residents formed a human chain to transfer books....

The opening of the Kimball Art Center rekindled community spirit. Show openings were community events, and the main gallery seemed second only to the local Post Office as a prime place for bumping into friends and catching up on gossip. Potters and photographers worked downstairs, and classes were held throughout the building.

Don Gomes was teaching guitar at the Kimball Art Center in 1978 when he convinced the Center's management to let him try some community theatre there. As an actor and director in stage and industrial shows before moving to Park City, Gomes had started a community theatre in Gilroy, California. After coming to Utah, he got involved in the graduate theatre program at the University of Utah. The thriving community theatre at the Kimball Art Center provided an outlet for amateur actors. Gradually, the smell of the greasepaint and roar of the crowd attracted residents from ski instructors to small businessmen to developers eager to explore their talents.

Staged in the gallery of the Kimball Art Center with rented risers to seat audiences of 150, the early shows weren't always smooth or easy. Typically, a telephone would ring on stage after an actor already was talking on it; or the lights would go up at the end of a scene, just as the actor who had just been killed was getting up and tiptoeing offstage.

The inaugural community theatre effort, *Cactus Flower*, didn't even attract many hopefuls to auditions, and Gomes had to start rehearsals without a lead actor. One evening he approached professional actor Lloyd Stevens on Main Street and insisted he accept the part. The cast also included local realtor Madeline Smith, who soon would become a staple in Park City theatre, singing, dancing, and acting in nearly every show to come. A school teacher, Brenda Bench, and a high school student, Tree Brown, also joined the cast along with Sidney Reed and Mary Ellen Wharton. If anyone was doubtful about how Park City would take to community theatre, they only needed to hear the ovation given Lloyd Stevens the minute he spoke his first line—a line delivered from off-stage.

Gomes hadn't meant to benefit from community theatre beyond the challenge and personal reward. But, after the first show, Teri Polson, a cub reporter from the *Park Record* introduced herself to him and requested an interview. Gomes suggested they conduct the discussion over a drink, and the next year they were married.

In fact, Teri Gomes played the most crucial role in the second production of what had become known as "Park City Players." The show, *Romanoff and Juliet*, was staged outdoors in the Kimball Art Center courtyard during summer of 1979. Nearby merchants balked at the idea of blocking traffic from the area, so the production was subject to honking horns, revving engines, and flashing headlights that scanned the stage. Teri appointed herself traffic cop, during curtain time, standing in front of the Art Center and directing traffic around the problem areas.

The second show again attracted a cadre of amateur performers whose names and faces would become familiar to community theatre audiences over the next five years: Chuck Folkerth, whose dog made an unscheduled walk on stage during one of the performances, Robin Riley, Kurt Graff, Susan Jarman, and Scott Graham. Stage manager David Fleisher acted in later productions and then became a script writer. Sunn Classics motion pictures, which was headquartered in Park City, where it filmed *Grizzly Adams* and other movies, donated costumes and even a professional wardrobe mistress, Heather Staley.

As the Park City Players continued, Gomes and the Art Center undertook more ambitious productions, such as *Oliver*, *Fiddler on the Roof*, *Camelot*, and *One Flew Over the Cuckoo's Nest*. Musicals also included dinner theatre performances at the Holiday Inn. Community theatre was so well received in Park City that a second group, Intermountain Actors Ensemble, entered production with shows such as *Wait Until Dark*, *Cat on a Hot Tin Roof*, *Once Upon a Mattress*, and *Bus Stop*.

In 1981, when the renovated Egyptian Theatre reopened, community theatre in Park City got a permanent home with a stage and seating that didn't have to be removed between performances. Intermountain

GROWING PAINS

P A R K   C I T Y

O.D. McGee: "The most important issue facing Park City is the dog issue. I would like to at least double the dog population. We are going to bus underprivileged dogs in from neighboring communities…"

S T I L L   C R A Z Y

PARK CITY

Actors Ensemble began summer Shakespeare productions at Park West.

Many of the amateurs who started with Park City Players even went on to professional acting. Dick Mitchell, who had been nearly dragged by friends to an audition for his first five-line community theatre part, went on to act in television advertisements and made-for-television movies. Ralph Carlson, first approached by Gomes to audition for *Camelot*, later starred as a fire-and-brimstone preacher in an Osmond Studio film. Steve Stanczyck starred in *Little Foxes*, *Cabaret*, and numerous other Park City productions before he joined a Shakespeare company in New York. Kathryn Haley who starred in *Peter Pan*, left for Hollywood soon after the final curtain.

Perhaps most near and dear to the hearts of the community theatre performers themselves was the initiation of an annual "Park City Academy Awards" ceremony (not to be confused with the annual theatre "Pot Gut Awards" developed for the local performers by *Park Record* theatre critic Rick Brough). Staged each year in similar fashion to the "real thing" Oscar ceremonies, the awards night included a host of "bests" in various categories, as voted by the individuals involved in community theatre. Numbers from the recent shows and numerous special awards generally were the most popular part of the ceremonies, such as the annual "Gum Dance With Me" award for truly dubious footwork in a musical performance. In fact, when Don Gomes awarded the "Gum Dance With Me" honor to local resident and aspiring performer Katy LaPay, she tripped and fell on her way up to the podium to receive her award.

"There were a lot of crazy times, tense times, and good times," Gomes says. "I saw so many people develop not only talent, but lasting friendships with one another.... Of course, there were times when everything was going wrong and I was sure my directing career was over. I remember *The Odd Couple* was so bad in dress rehearsal that I didn't even want to be seen opening night. I just slid way down in a chair in the very back. I was wrong of course. It turned out to be a terrific production...."

Another kind of production that has allowed Parkites an opportunity to vent the ham in their souls is the annual Snowflaker's Ball. A costume party fund raiser for the Chamber of Commerce and Convention and Visitors Bureau, the event takes place in November, but the hype starts much earlier. One of the late 1970s balls, for example, had a "Godfather" theme, prompting various town notables to appoint themselves as feuding "dons," whose families had their ultimate showdown at Snowflaker's Ball. A life-size Park City Monopoly game was the focal point of another ball, with various organizations and businesses signing up to form the teams that would play the game. The team tokens sent around the giant board ranged from the bikini-clad reigning Mr. Utah (the token of an all-female team), to a toilet on wheels, to a four-foot high remote-controlled martini glass.

On April 1, when the need to get crazy strikes again, at the end of long winter, Parkites don clown costumes for a dress-up day at the Park City Ski Area. "Clown Day" quickly grew beyond clowns and beyond the ski area, with a general Halloween atmosphere permeating the town. Gorillas, hobos, ducks, and clowns flock to the slopes for some downhill runs in between general partying and dancing that lasts well into the night.

Not surprisingly, Parkites also continued their long and dearly held tradition of making their own good times. For example, Deworth Williams, an investment advisor, and Don Griffin, a real estate agent, became skiing pals who always were prepared for some creative fun and pranks on the slopes. Local legend has it that some of their best times were spent posing as ski instructors, often to eliminate waiting by simply joining the front of a lift line and calling, "Ski school, ski school!" This also led to the novel idea of taking struggling beginning skiers under their wings and encouraging them down difficult slopes. The experiences proved hair-raising, but certainly memorable, for the unsuspecting novices who found themselves facing high moguls on steep runs.

Williams even attempted sport on the slopes one summer by driving his pickup truck up the steeply pitching "Gotcha" ski run. Halfway up, the truck seemed about to topple backwards over on to itself; however, it did manage to survive, thanks to an eleventh-hour decision to nudge it all the way around for the harrowing downhill run home.

No matter how many significant events and ongoing activities got their start during the 1970s, the second half of the decade will be remembered as the time of the great land grab. Suddenly, Park City property was "hot," and there were millions to be made in buying it and building on it.

Mary Lehmer: "When the resort first opened, there was more activity here than Park City's ever seen since. Every other door was the swinging door of a bar or a restaurant, and people really knew how to have fun...."

STILL CRAZY

PARK CITY

The old farms and ranchlands on the outskirts of town were ripe for development into suburban communities for families who were moving in from all over the nation. Closer to the ski slopes, condominiums began to spring up at a relentless pace, providing lodging for tourists and second home owners and a quick return on investment for developers. On Main Street, new office buildings replaced the smaller, cruder structures that had housed early shops and businesses.

The development boom even took hold in the original residential district, which had come to be known as "Old Town" (but which old timers still insisted actually was Park City, with everything else being "New Town"). Miners' cabins and Victorian-trimmed bungalows soon were subject to stiff competition from duplexes, triplexes, and even eight-plexes lining the steep roads that terraced up the hills beyond Main Street.

Developers arrived from California, Salt Lake City, and points in between to push for new zoning and new land uses that would make a profitable undertaking even more profitable. Many Park City residents joined in; for awhile it seemed everyone in town aspired to become a real estate agent, while every real estate agent aspired to become a developer. There was a planning commission and a "master plan", and there was a city administration, but no entity was prepared to deal with the rapid, runaway growth and the fever-pitch building boom that enveloped the town.

"In some cases, things were just happening too fast; in other cases, we were just too naive" said former planning commissioner Roy Reynolds. He recalled the Depot Project, adjacent to the northern end of Main Street, as one of the worst mistakes made while he served on Planning Commission: "It was proposed to us as a really impressive development that would restore and utilize the old Victorian Union Pacific train depot and add brick walkways, elegant old railroad cars as lodging, a hotel, ponds, and heavy landscaping. We got caught up in the charisma of the major development partner, Wally Wright, who had done a beautiful job on the development of Trolley Square in Salt Lake City."

As Reynolds explained it, the several acres of land involved had a variety of zoning. The developer requested higher density historic commercial zoning, although the proposed project wouldn't utilize the full density available. "We got carried away and rezoned the whole area," said Reynolds. "Next thing we knew, the partnership dissolved and the new owner came in with new plans—a mammoth square brick condominium hotel that utilized the zoning we'd granted to its maximum. Forget the landscaping, ponds and walkways." Two square, four-story brick buildings soon towered over the small, surrounding houses. Meanwhile, the old railroad deposit still stood empty and unrestored five years later.

Said city planner Bill Ligety on the project: "It's a perfect example of the type of development that could and did happen when the city changes zoning to a classification that isn't what's wanted, because it's convinced that the developer only will build what really is wanted. Once the zoning has changed, no matter how good intentions are, people will build to the maximum."

No one in Park City could have imagined the pressures and impacts of the 1970s building boom. While the 1966 Master Plan for the town had set forth the objective of preserving "the mining town appearance of Park City", it avoided any specification of what constituted a "mining town appearance." It certainly did not contemplate the annexations on the north side of town that quickly doubled the city's land area.

When a new city manager, Arlene Loble, arrived in 1980, she found what she later referred to as, "A community that simply hadn't been prepared to manage the growth that was happening to it." New developments ranged anywhere from exemplary to questionable. Some valuable city land parcels had been sold to developers, and some interesting old buildings had been demolished. There also were still no street signs in Old Town.

By 1980, a question being asked by many Parkites was, "Can Park City survive the 1970s?" In fact, there were some very real indications that it could, and a lot of people even saw a good portion of silver lining in the changes that had taken place. City services were improving, and there was a greater choice of housing than ever before. There were tennis courts, golf courses, and even a free bus system. A new Holiday Inn, shopping mall, and supermarket indicated that planning could incorporate a certain amount of sensitivity. A new ski area, Deer Valley, was being developed with appropriate attention to its impact on the land and the nearby residents. As Harry Reed said "If you look at Main Street now, compared to when I first

> Deworth Williams attempted sport on the slopes one summer by driving his pick-up truck up the steeply pitching "Gotcha" ski run....Halfway up, the truck seemed about to topple backwards....

LAND GRAB

PARK CITY

When a new city manager, Arlene Loble, arrived in 1980, she found what she later referred to as, "A community that simply hadn't been prepared to manage the growth that was happening to it."

moved here, you'd have to say that a lot of changes have been for the better. There are fewer vacant lots, and fewer boarded up buildings with their roofs falling in. The whole street is a lot cleaner now."

Oddly enough, while development boomed through the 1970s, a spirit of preservation also began to occur. At a time when rising land values seemed to favor demolishing the old structures and starting over, citizen and government endeavors got underway to preserve the most significant portions of what remained. A "Historic District" was defined in 1978, and a Historic District Commission was formed to draft guidelines on everything from signs to structural scale within its boundaries. Individual residents, the city government, and even developers started to take a renewed interest in restoring and preserving older homes and buildings.

In the forefront of many efforts to save some larger buildings was Tina Lewis, who had arrived in Park City in the mid-1970s and was elected to City Council in 1979. Lewis got the idea that the old, boarded up Miners Hospital, an elegant brick structure when it was built in 1904, might make an ideal home for a new city library. Funding for the project came when citizens approved renovation financing in a city bond election—although in the same election they turned down the financing of a new sports arena, a field house, and park improvements. When the library opened, more than 700 residents formed a human chain to transfer all books one mile from the old library to the new structure.

Lewis's next project was pushing through a restoration of the 1885 City Hall on Main Street, a project scheduled for completion in Park City's centennial year. These examples of governmental preservation efforts seemed to give impetus to private investment in the same direction. "I never thought I'd hear it," Lewis said, "but some developers around town are talking about the need to preserve old buildings."

Indeed, by 1981, the development group Silver Mill of Park City had purchased and restored the Egyptian Theatre, not only returning it to its original Egyptian Revival motif, but also enlarging its lobby and installing new light and sound equipment. Bob Lewis, a developer from Virginia who frequently came to ski, bought and restored the 1897 Mormon church on Park Avenue, adapting it to condominiums as the Blue Church Lodge. When it was nearly completely gutted by fire, Lewis rebuilt the lodge, retaining the spirit of the old church by once again restoring its high arched window shapes and steeply pitched roof. The Washington School, which had been constructed in 1889, sat abandoned for years before developer Mac MacQuoid decided to save it and turn it into bed-and-breakfast lodging.

Unfortunately, not all the notable early structures survived long enough to become candidates for preservation. Fire has plagued Park City since its earliest days, claiming numerous homes and public buildings. The most tragic of recent blazes struck in the summer of 1982 at the Silver King Coalition Mines building on Park Avenue. The eight-story frame structure at the terminal of the tramway that hauled ore from the mountain had towered over Park City for 80 years, its sweeping height and diagonal cross beams reminding residents and visitors of the town's heritage. Images of the building appeared on postcards, posters, T-shirts, and logos of many Park City businesses and organizations. For many years, it was the symbol of Park City.

One July evening, three men from Salt Lake City who were in the area to attend a concert scaled the surrounding barbed wire fence and broke into the empty Coalition building. Growing chilly, they gathered together some wood shavings and planking to build a fire on the wooden floor of the all-wood building. The blaze soon was seen from as far away as Snyderville. Although nearby windows shattered and paint melted off parked cars, no other buildings caught fire. Dr. Patrick Sweeney, whose family owned the structure, expressed the sentiment of the entire community the next day: "It's like losing a member of the family." The men who started the destruction fared better, receiving suspended sentences on misdemeanor charges.

Among the numerous residential renovations, the Raddon house on Park Avenue, which was built by *Park Record* editor/publisher Sam Raddon, is most noteworthy. Former mayor John Price and his wife Nicky purchased the three-story, 11-room home as a virtual shell, with no electricity or plumbing. The house had been uninhabited for 20 years, but, after seven months of strenuous fulltime work, and approximately $30,000 in materials, the home was transformed into what may be the most striking Victorian residence in Park City.

SETTLING DOWN

PARK CITY

Next door to the Raddon house, Marion Lintner turned a 1907 Lutheran church into a home for herself and her two daughters. Replacing antique stained glass windows and leaving the high church ceiling open, she managed to preserve the original look while adding a bedroom balcony and small alcove kitchen. One of the most astounding renovations of an Old Town residence was executed by Lessing Stern on the crude miner's cabin he bought on Woodside Avenue. The structure that had been a box-like ramshackle shell just a few years before suddenly took on near mansion proportions, complete with custom inlaid wood floors, a greenhouse, solar panels, and a 12-foot long Jacuzzi.

While preservation caught on in Old Town, the boom in new building also was far from played out. Royal Street, which had sold its existing ski facilities to Alpine Meadows, unveiled an ambitious new plan for the acreage it had retained in Deer Valley. During the late 1970s and into the 1980s, construction got underway on the next Royal Street venture, Deer Valley Resort. Determined to make the ski area a luxury experience for all who visited it, Royal Street spent $20 million before the first lift opened in 1981. Sporting impeccably groomed ski runs, gourmet food in the lodges, and both elegant condominiums and single-family home sites selling for up to $200,000, Deer Valley also added popular Stein Eriksen as director of skiing.

Meanwhile, the Park City Ski Area, unwilling to rest on its laurels, continued to cut new runs and build new lifts; in 1984, it even began plans for a "town lift" that would carry local skiers from a central location in Old Town to the very center of the ski area. Another new 12.5-acre project called Park City Village brought a maze of shops, restaurants, condominiums and an ice rink to the base of the main ski area.

For community-conscious citizens, there always seemed to be a new event or undertaking. One of the most enduring of these was the inception of a Park City radio station, KPCW, in 1981. Station director Blair Feulner was largely responsible for making KPCW happen, relying on individual contributions and business underwriting to develop community, not commercial, radio. Dozens of local volunteers were trained in radio broadcast techniques and took enthusiastically to the airwaves as disc jockeys, newscasters, and talk-show hosts. Weekly shows were put on the air by local people such as the police chief, an architect, an art gallery owner, and a federal government employee.

Among the new personalities who soon emerged from KPCW were: Two Ton Tillie, whose on-the-air recipes were even more fun to hear about than to cook; Old Bill, who graced the air with homespun wisdom acquired through—by his own estimate—about 90 years in the mines; and The Shaft, Park City's own Rona Barrett, whose calling was to share "truths and trivia from the tunnels of local gossip" with her "dear, dear listeners."

What kind of people have been willing to invest their time, energy, and money in a Park City full of colossal growing pains, problems and risks, and headed toward uncertain change? The people who moved in and made Park City home have hailed from all walks of life, all professions, and all parts of the nation. Some came to make money, some to make new careers, some to make an escape from whatever wasn't right about Los Angeles, Chicago, or Salt Lake City. The result soon became an eclectic population not dissimilar in motivation or aspiration from those who arrived to join the silver boom a century earlier.

Don and Beverly Maw, for example, are not uncharacteristic. They fell in love with Park City on a ski vacation and soon left their jobs in Detroit. After researching business possibilities in the area, Don began a new career as owner and manager of Holiday Rental Cars in Salt Lake City. Similarly, Don and Eleanor Griffin came from California to ski and soon moved to Park City with their two children, even though they had no idea what they would do to make a living. Ultimately, Don settled on work in real

SETTLING DOWN

estate, while Eleanor pursued her career in physical therapy with a county agency.

For others, Park City was a career move. Arlene Loble was an assistant city manager in Connecticut and thought that someday she'd want to manage a town such as Steamboat Springs, Colorado. When she came to Park City to interview for the job as city manager, she immediately knew she'd found the right place. Debby Symonds, executive director of the Chamber of Commerce/Convention and Visitors Bureau, was a sales executive at Hotel Utah in Salt Lake City when she was offered a job as sales director at the new Park City Holiday Inn.

A growing group of Parkites were able to move to the mountains without ever leaving their jobs in other places. The long-haul commuters include airline pilots who ranged from Bob Powers, based in Dallas, to Vince Donile, based in Chicago. They also include Betty Brown, an actress who commutes to her work in Los Angeles, and Tom Mathews, who calls his Deer Valley residence home but travels to Washington, D.C., to tend to his business partnership in high-level fund raising. Chickie McAllister is away from Park City and his family for at least a month at a time when he goes to work on an oil rig in the North Sea. Similarly, Scott Abrams commutes from Park City to work on the seas, in his case as a Merchant Marine Officer.

Good times for vacationers on the ski slopes also brought numerous second home owners to Park City, many of them familiar faces from television and movies. Hal Linden, television's *Barney Miller*, and his wife Fran bought a Park City home and became regulars in many community causes. Linden donated his name and talent to act as master of ceremonies for the gala opening of the renovated Egyptian Theatre. Kate Jackson, of *Charlie's Angels* fame, bought a home in Park City, as did television and film actors David and Meredith Baxter Birney.

The Park City of the 1980s is a long way from Park City of the 1880s. Its economic base has progressed from silver to snow, and its populace has progressed from arrival in wooden wagons to arrival by moving companies. Homes are more substantial, streets are more permanent, and summers are more entertaining now. But, the residents themselves may not be so very different. They still worry about the future of their families and their jobs, as well as about schools and taxes. They still are surrounded by various measures of doubt, optimism, hard work, hard play, joy, and sorrow.

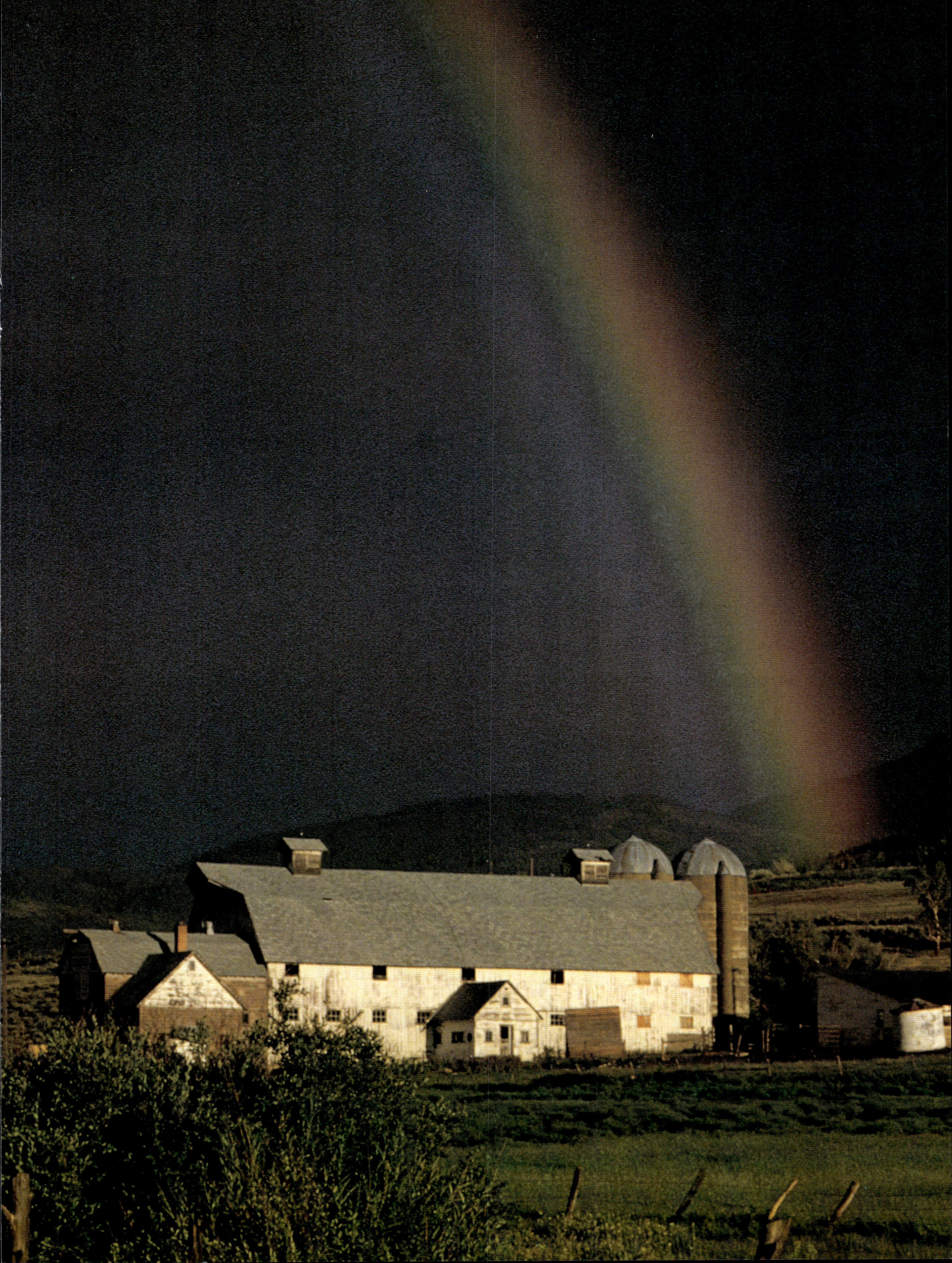

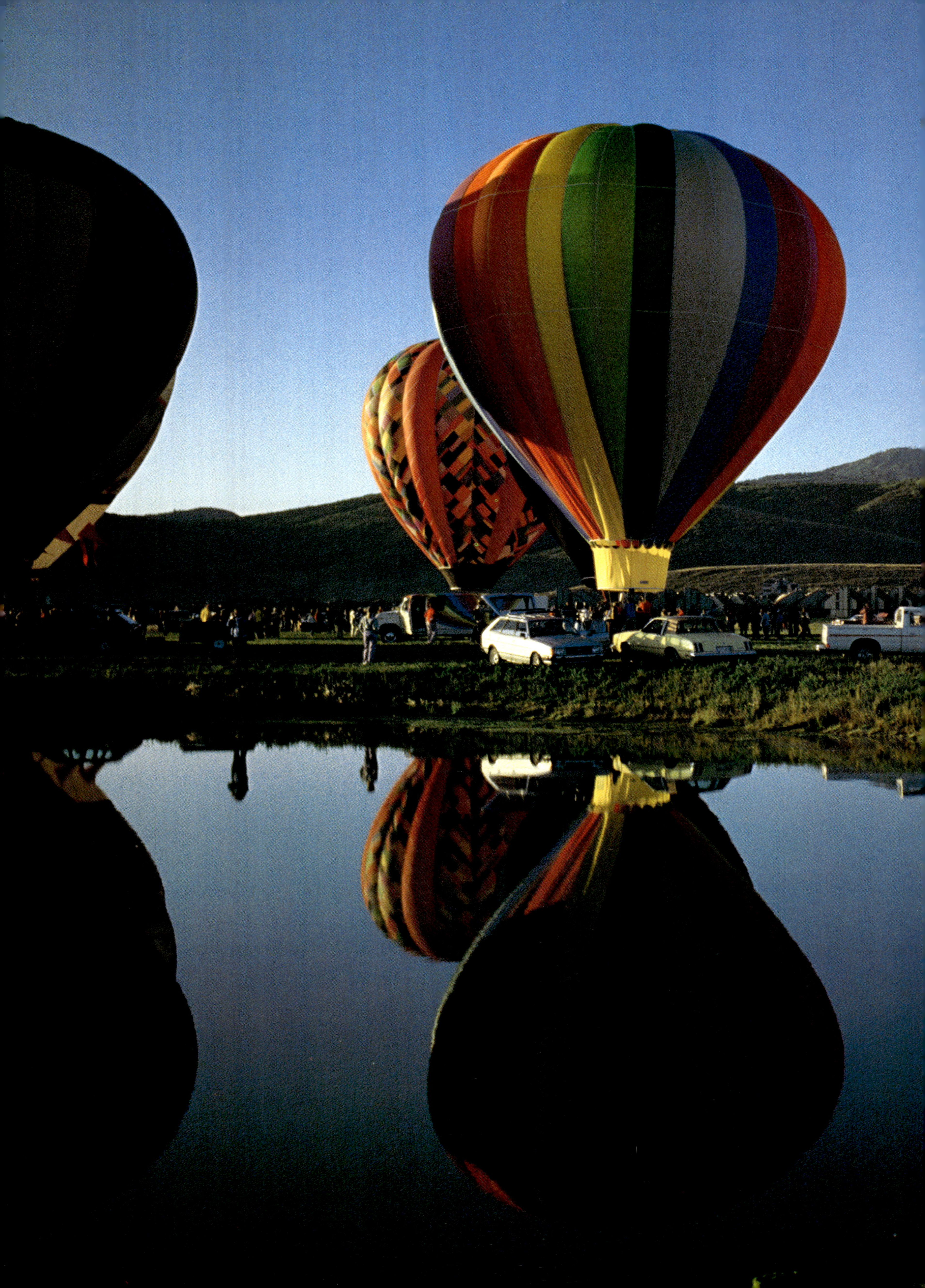

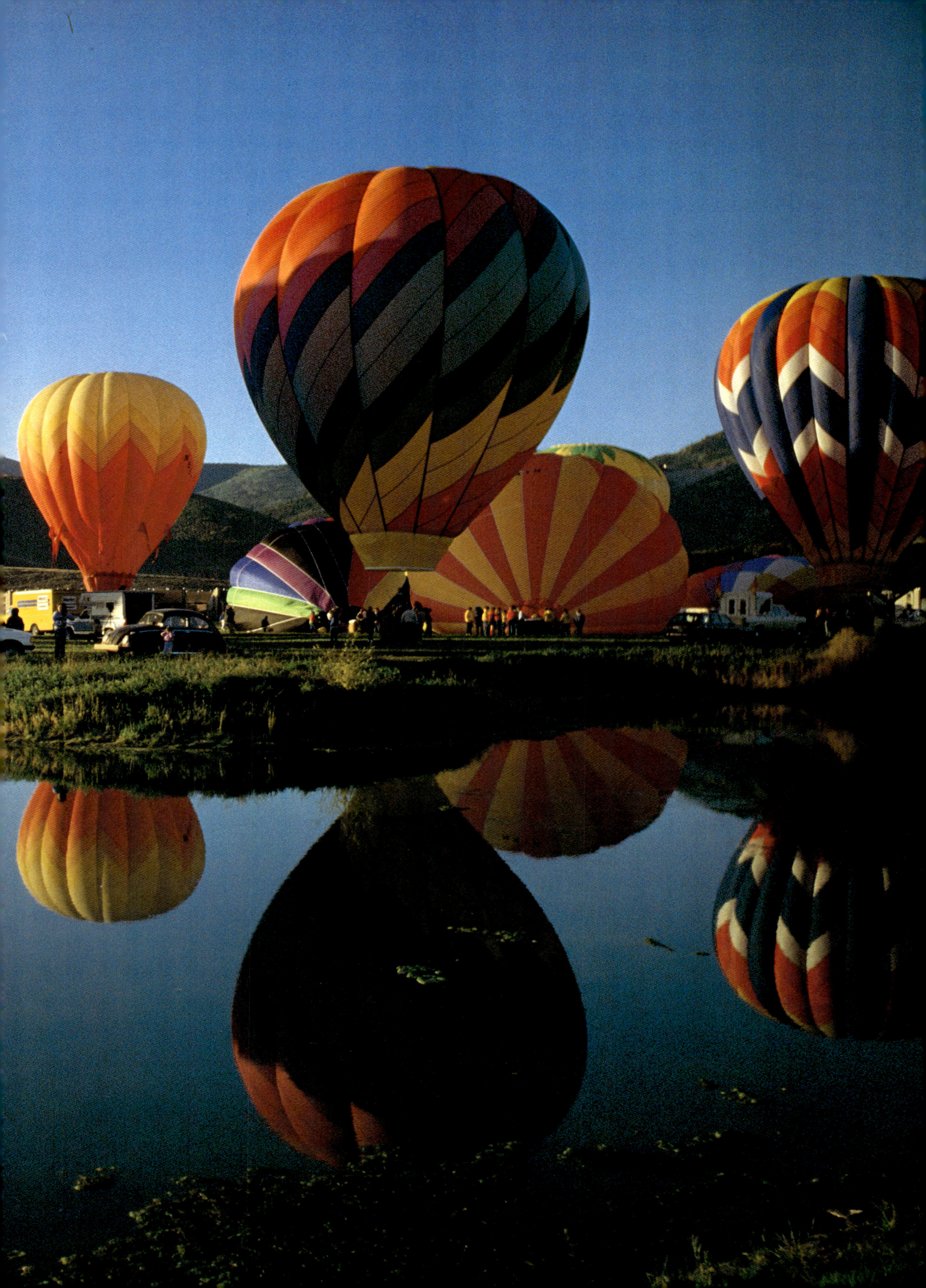

PARK CITY

WARM AND WET

P A R K   C I T Y

From racing on horseback or bicycle to skimming across a reservoir or a rugby field, locals and visitors alike find plenty of summer activity.

W A R M   A N D   W E T

PARK CITY

COUNTRY ROADS

PARK CITY

FLORA

P A R K C I T Y

Wildlife abounds throughout the Wasatch and nearby Uinta Mountains. Eagles soar above the aspens, while deer and rabbits drink at sparkling mountain lakes.

F A U N A

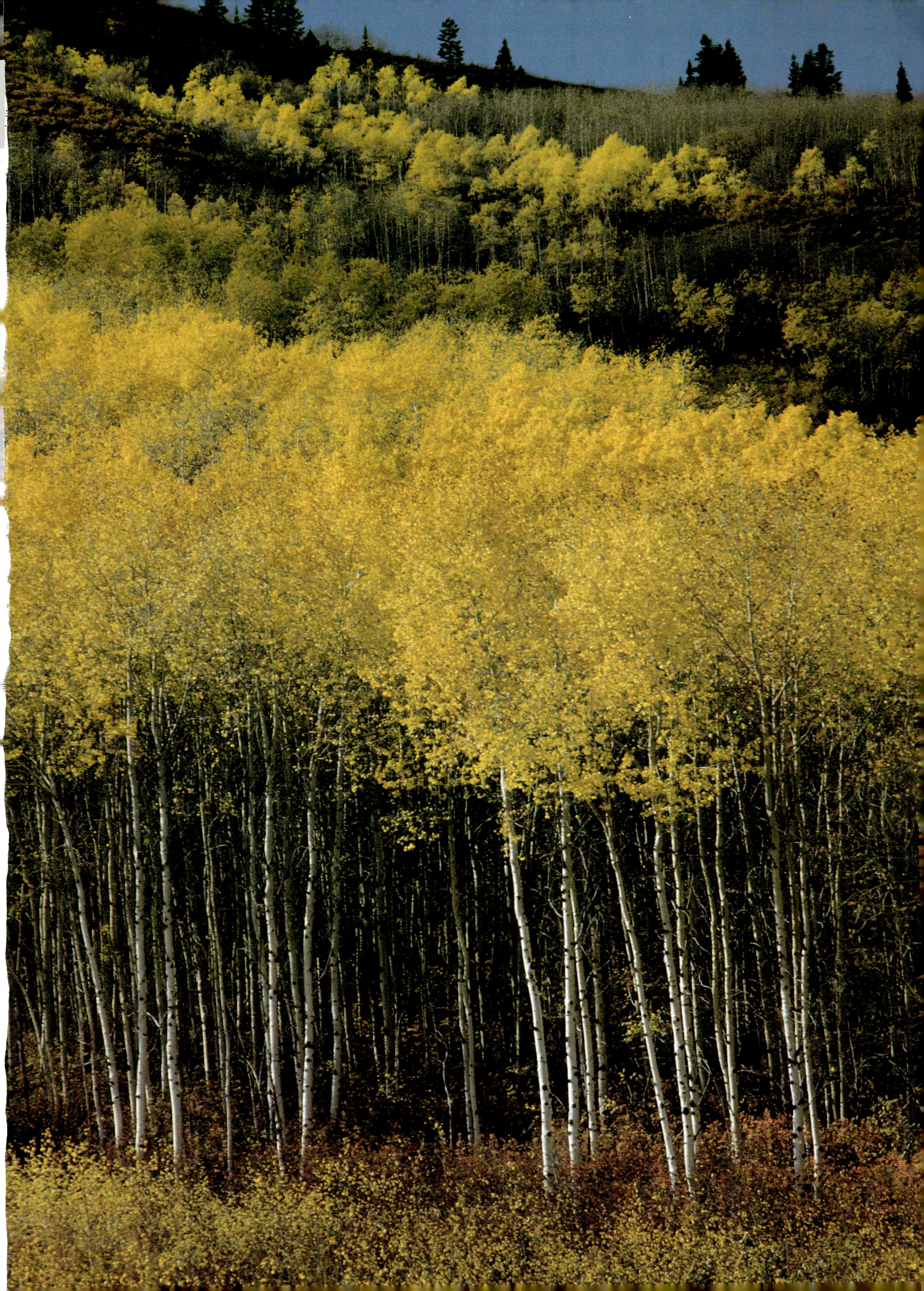

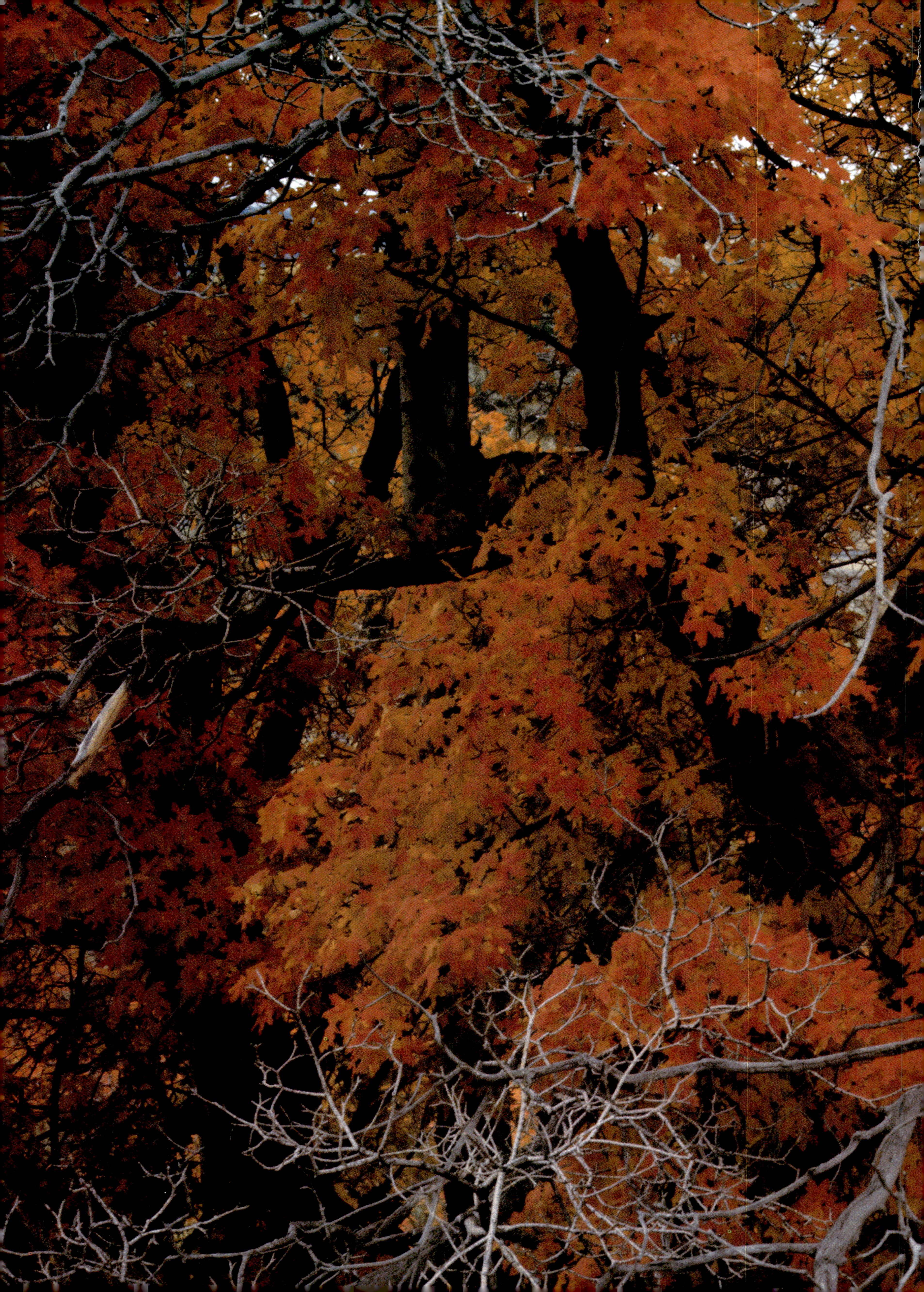

P A R K C I T Y

T H I N K S N O W